So You've Landed
in a Fantasy World

So You've Landed in a Fantasy World

How to Survive and Thrive

Josiah Lebowitz

McFarland & Company, Inc., Publishers

Jefferson, North Carolina

All drawings are by Ye Sun Kim

ISBN (print) 978–1-4766–8527–4
ISBN (ebook) 978–1-4766–4499–8

Library of Congress and British Library
cataloguing data are available

Front cover image of portal in forest: Shutterstock/nur hafidiatama

Printed in the United States of America

*McFarland & Company, Inc., Publishers
Box 611, Jefferson, North Carolina 28640
www.mcfarlandpub.com*

To all the residents of Earth who, after
finding themselves in a strange new world,
bravely took up their swords, shields, and spatulas
to fight monsters, demons, and bad cuisine.
And also, to the writers who shared their stories
with us so we can better prepare
the next generation of heroes.

Praise for This Guide

"Goddesses are useless and party members with major personality quirks are best avoided? I knew I should have read this sooner."

—K. Satou

"I almost want to return by death and do everything over again just so I can follow the advice in this book."

—S. Natsuki

"A wonderful treasure trove of advice. Especially the part about not accepting candy from witches."

—E. Pevensie

"From its warnings about betrayal to its praise of raccoon girls, this book contains everything a summoned hero should know."

—N. Iwatani

"A game isn't something you play. You need to know how to live, fight, and survive. This guide will set you on that path."

—K. Kirigaya

"Wear clothes. Damn! Why didn't I think of that?"

—S. Yoshida

"Be careful. Be cautious. Be overly cautious. Read *So You've Landed in a Fantasy World*. Then, for sure, you'll prove that you can save your friends, your loved ones, and the entire world."

—S. Ryuuguuin

Table of Contents

Praise for This Guide   vi

Acknowledgments   ix

Everyone's Going to Fantasy Worlds   xi

1. That Time I Somehow Ended Up in a Fantasy World   1

2. Be Prepared   9

3. You Made It! Now What?   22

4. First Things First   34

5. Rising of an Isekai Hero   41

6. Combat and You   48

7. Magical Me   58

8. Gearing Up   65

9. Forming Your Party   73

10. Surviving and Thriving in a Standard Fantasy World   86

11. Not Being Made a Fool of in a Comic Fantasy World   95

12. Pwning a Video Game Fantasy World   103

13. Hopelessly Trying to Stay Alive in a Dark Fantasy World   112

14. Otherworldly Romance   122

15. Kingdom Building 101   130

Table of Contents

16. How an Earthly Hero Saved the World   138

17. Now What?   145

18. Homeward Bound   153

19. It's Never Over ... Unless It Is   160

Additional Research Material   169

Index   179

Acknowledgments

So You've Guides* would like to thank Professor Josiah Lebowitz for his tireless work studying and analyzing the countless trials and travails of the many, many heroes who have, through one method or another, found themselves starting over in a fantasy world. The data he collected, trends he identified, and strategies he formulated were vital to the creation of this guide. If any fantasy worlds are looking for a strong, intelligent hero to save the day, we highly recommend him (especially since our royalty agreement doesn't extend to residents of the fantasyverse).

Credit also goes to his editor, Elizabeth Siebold, for her many tips and suggestions, including pointing out all the misplaced commas, dangling sentences, and other niggling issues that most people probably would have just overlooked anyway. And to our illustrator, Ye Sun Kim, for the many intelligent and insightful (or perhaps just ridiculous) drawings found throughout this guide. And who can forget our helpful beta readers including Brian, Gen ... and all those other people whose names we forgot.

We would also like to thank the fine folks at McFarland for partnering with us to bring this guide to market, with extra special thanks to Layla Milholen for her efforts. Their aid has ensured that future generations of heroes will arrive in the fantasyverse far better prepared than ever before.

In addition, we wish to acknowledge K. Satou, S.

---

* So You've Guides (the publisher and guidebook series) does not currently exist on Earth, at least not in this dimension or timeline. But it should, and hopefully will once we get all the temporal disturbances worked out. In the meantime, we are proud to partner with the fine folks at McFarland to help you prepare for any upcoming adventures in the fantasyverse.

Acknowledgments

Natsuki, D. Gale, S. Ryuguin, K. Higurashi, and the many other Earthborn heroes of the fantasyverse who have protected, and continue to protect, both their worlds and ours from destruction.

Finally, we would like to thank you, the readers. We hope that your own adventures in the fantasyverse are exciting, successful, and, above all, lots of fun (while featuring minimal amounts of despair, dismemberment, and demonic slugs). Remember, no matter what sort of fantastical situation you may find yourself in, So You've Guides is here to help. See you on the other side!

Everyone's Going
to Fantasy Worlds

Today, it seems as if everyone from heroic-yet-angsty teenagers, to giggling schoolgirls, to bored middle-aged businessmen, to attractive housewives, are finding themselves whisked away to save distant worlds from some kind of unspeakable evil. But how do you prepare for such an amazing adventure? Fortunately, we're here to help. While other guidebook makers are content with helping you learn how to build a website or balance a budget, only we at So You've Guides help you overcome life's greatest and most exciting trials. For decades we've been the company you turn to when you find yourself stalked by a serial killer, solving a ghastly murder, or navigating a needlessly complex love triangle. But we know that you, our readers, are now facing challenges that are increasingly fantastical in nature, taking you far beyond the bounds of Earth to traverse space, time, and even other dimensions. To that end, we have worked hard to prepare the volume you now hold in your hands (or stare at on your screen).

So You've Landed in a Fantasy World has been developed based on the input of numerous heroes who have traveled to magical lands and returned to tell the tale, as analyzed and compiled by Professor Josiah Lebowitz, novelist, travel writer, game designer, and leading expert in the field of Isekaiology. In these pages you'll learn how to increase (or, if you prefer, decrease) your chances of successfully being chosen. You can also find useful advice to help you prepare for your eventual trip and hit the ground running once you arrive. While the success and survival rate of summoned heroes is surprisingly high, a little preparation can make your new life much easier. And, of course, we'll also help you decide what to do after your adventures have ended.

So, when the time comes for you to take your place as a sword-wielding slime fighting evil and rebuilding a kingdom alongside your overpowered mother, we hope that you'll join our countless other satisfied customers and turn to So You've Guides to prepare you for this, and all the other strange, mysterious, and fantastical challenges you may face.

≒ 1 ≒

That Time I
Somehow Ended Up
in a Fantasy World

So you want to live in a fantasy world and go on epic adventures with a party of cool and attractive girls and/or guys? Well, you're in luck! The likelihood that you'll be summoned to, or reincarnated into, a fantasy world is rapidly rising. The fantasyverse has become so desperate for heroes that fantasy worlds have significantly reduced their requirements, and are now searching for potential heroes of all ages, skills, and experience levels. And why wouldn't you want to go? Adventure, heroism, treasure, cute cat girls, handsome dog boys! The fantasyverse has them all. Are you ready? Well, while there are no guarantees, taking advantage of as many of the following situations as possible will significantly increase your odds of being chosen.

On the flipside, if you're one of those rare individuals who would rather live out the entirety of their lives peacefully on Earth, enjoying modern conveniences like the internet, TV, central heating, air conditioning, and indoor plumbing, then avoid the following scenarios like the plague. While a trip to the fantasyverse still isn't entirely outside of the realm of possibility, at least you'll have tried.

Having the Right Attitude

Before trying to trigger the right situation for a trip to the fantasyverse, it's best to take stock of your own personality. Determined, heroic individuals (even if that heroism is buried deep within their psyche) with a strong sense of justice are the preferred choice of fantasy worlds everywhere. So working hard to cultivate those qualities in yourself will only boost your chances.

Unsurprisingly, the fantasyverse abhors assholes. So, if you would rather ensure that you remain on Earth, becoming the world's biggest douchebag is a reasonable approach. But you'll really have to commit to the role, as a jerk with a heart of gold is just begging for a heartwarming redemption arc. Do note, however, that this strategy is not without its risks as if, against all odds, you still end up in a fantasy world, you'll soon discover that karma is a bitch. At best, you'll be reborn in some sort of embarrassing, and possibly not even human, form. At worst, you'll be painfully tortured and/or killed shortly after arrival.

However, it's worth mentioning that there have been a handful of recently reported cases of the fantasyverse recruiting people from Earth to fill the role of dark lords and other villains. While this is still relatively

If, for some reason, you really DON'T want to go to a fantasy world, becoming a major douchebag will significantly lower your chances.

rare, we here at So You've Guides are monitoring the situation and will be preparing a new guide (*So You've Decided to Brutally Conquer a Fantasy World*) for any would be kings or queens of darkness.

The Family Connection

Perhaps the most surefire way to end up in a fantasy world is to be related to someone who went there before. Do you have an estranged uncle who rambles on about dragons and magic? Perhaps a grandmother who often looks at the stars and sighs while grasping an ancient pendant? Maybe a parent or sibling who mysteriously disappeared when you were young? If so, you'd better pack your bags, because it's only a matter of time before you're whisked away to pick up where they left off.

To ensure that you're the one chosen, as opposed to some other less deserving relative, be sure to show a significant interest in everything that family member says. Ask lots of questions, listen to all of his or her stories, and always BELIEVE. For bonus points, try and get your relative to give you some sort of relic or talisman from the other world, and keep it on your person at all times.

Do keep in mind that, in these situations, you'll often be called upon to deal with any unfinished business said relative may have left behind. Make sure you're aware of any star-crossed lovers, surviving enemies, or uncompleted quests to avoid getting caught off-guard.

Finding a Warp Zone

There are many ways to end up in a fantasy world, but one of the more popular do-it-yourself options is to find some sort of magical portal hidden in the "real" world. While you may expect such portals to exist in the depths of crumbling temples or the darkest reaches of an ancient forest, they can also turn up in much more mundane and easily reached locations.

Mysterious books, perhaps tucked in a dusty forgotten corner of the local library, often serve as gateways to other worlds. Or, at very least, may introduce you to a world of magic operating in secret here on Earth (if that happens to you, please see our upcoming guide on surviving and thriving in an urban fantasy, *So You've Discovered That Magic*

Was Real All Along). Just make absolutely certain not to free any beings who might be sealed inside said books; they're almost certainly evil and will only make your new life far more dangerous and complicated than it needs to be.

Portals can also be found at the bottom of wells, particularly those that sit in locations surrounded by mystery or charged with spiritual power. Just make sure to wear a swimsuit and prepare a rope you can use to climb back out if your well of choice ends up being one of the more ordinary variety.

Mirrors are a classic choice too, especially if they're old and extremely ornate, and even more so if they're engraved with strange letters or runes. Be on the lookout for fleeting glimpses of figures that you can't quite make out, or reflections of objects or even entire locations

Unfortunately, not all wells double as portals to the fantasyverse.

4

that aren't there. Though, if you do find yourself being pulled into a mirror, keep in mind that there's a moderate chance that, instead of a fantasy world, you'll find yourself trapped in a mirror dimension, often while an evil doppelganger takes your place back in reality. Warning your friends and family about the possibility, and carrying around an (ideally magical) item with a strong connection to your home should help you escape if needed. Or, if all else fails, don't underestimate the power of a good hammer.

No mention of easily accessible portals would be complete without talking about wardrobes. Ideally the wardrobe should be old and made of the wood from an ancient and mysterious tree that grew from a magic seed, or blossomed year-round. Just open the door, push past the surprisingly large collection of coats you're certain to find inside, and away you go. You should, however, be aware that portals of this type tend to be rather inconsistent, appearing or disappearing based on the time of day, who is looking, and when would be the most inconvenient and/or embarrassing for the user.

If none of the previously listed locations pan out, don't give up. There's really no place that a magical portal won't appear if the conditions are right. Chase rainbows, crawl into caves and rabbit holes, answer ringing payphones, and squeeze down large green pipes. As long as you keep at it, you're almost guaranteed to find a portal sooner or later.

For SCIENCE!

Science experiments frequently result in strange and unexpected phenomena, including the generation of portals to other dimensions. Be sure to volunteer as a test subject and/or lab assistant for as many experiments as possible, particularly those related to teleportation, other dimensions, strange creatures, and particle acceleration. Though, if you're dead set on going to a fantasy world, and only a fantasy world, you may want to avoid this method as it could also result in time travel, alien abduction, or the unleashing of unspeakable cosmic horrors, which will then have to be banished back to the hellscape from which they came (in the latter case, run to your nearest bookstore and purchase a copy of *So You've Somehow Summoned Cthulhu* before it's too late). On that same note, be absolutely certain to avoid any experiments involving genetic or bio engineering, mutations, or the like, as they rarely generate portals and are most likely to result in either super powers (good, but not a trip to a fantasy world), or the zombie apocalypse (very bad). Finally, any experiments that result in melting green bananas should be halted as quickly as possible in order to prevent CERN's planned takeover of the Earth.

If you'd rather avoid the risks inherent with experimental science, you may instead want to focus your efforts on video games. Online VR games are the most likely to result in a trip to the fantasyverse, but any game can do, especially if it's brand new, experimental, and/or otherwise mysterious. To have the greatest chance of success, you'll need to ensure that you're playing the game at particularly auspicious times such as its launch, the release of any new expansions, and, for online games, when the servers are inevitably shut down. Choose your game carefully, as you'll most likely end up inside its world, and quite possibly stuck in the body of your avatar. And be warned that half the time you won't be physically transported to the game world, but will instead find your mind trapped in the game while your body slowly wastes away back in reality. Be sure to make arrangements ahead of time for the retrieval and care of your body to avoid becoming a literal ghost in the machine.

Be the Very Best, Like No One Ever Was

These days, the fantasyverse isn't especially picky about who it summons, but it is occasionally on the lookout for individuals with exceptional skills. If you're a champion gamer, fencer, martial artist, sprinter, singer, or the like, your chances of getting summoned have just gone way up. Do note that some skills are more valuable than others, especially those that can be applied to combat or magic. So far, there are no known cases of world champion knitters or hot dog eaters being summoned, but don't despair. The way things are going, it may just be a matter of time. The fantasyverse seems to be undergoing an extreme shortage of workers in a variety of fields, so even skilled reporters, middle managers, and delivery boys may find themselves receiving a call.

On the flip side, some fantasy worlds thrive on irony so, if you don't find yourself with any particularly strong skills that you can leverage, you may be able to increase your odds by being so painfully average and boring that there's no good reason why anyone would ever summon you.

Winning the Isekai Lottery

Sometimes, you just get lucky. Or unlucky, as the case may be. Just cross your fingers and see what happens. Fate, the gods, or some other cosmic force might just happen to pick you out at random. As a note, unless you have a penchant for real life murder games, we recommend avoiding any luck-based invitations to super elite high schools.

Death—The Final Resort

If all else fails, don't give up yet. Quite a lot of heroes end up in a fantasy world only after their untimely demise. *Please remember that being transported to, or reborn in a fantasy world (or any other world) after death is by no means guaranteed. As such, So You've Guides strongly discourages any attempts to intentionally invoke this situation.* Besides, heroic deaths, brought upon by saving another from getting stabbed or being run over by a truck, are by far the most likely to attract the notice of the fantasyverse. As such, it's best to think of the possibility of being reborn in a fantasy world after death as a potential bonus, rather than something to actively strive for.

If you do, through some very unfortunate turn of events, find yourself dying, keep in mind that your final actions, words, and/or thoughts can have a large effect on where you'll end up and what type of skills, or even body, you'll have upon arrival. While you may be able to keep your own body (magically healed from any and all injuries, and likely granted some sort of special power), you might also be reborn or reincarnated into a new form. So be prepared to suddenly find yourself switching genders, gaining wings, growing tentacles, or even turning into some type of amorphous blob. It's therefore recommended that you carefully plan out your last words and thoughts in advance, and immediately launch into them if you ever feel that the end is near. Focus particularly on how strong and smart you want to be, along with what type of powers or skills you would like to have. Final words or thoughts such as, "in my next life, I wish I could be a brilliant swordsman (or swordswoman, if you prefer) with impenetrable skin" will likely have a far better result than "I can't believe I'm so stupid that I got run over by a delivery bike." That said, do note that your reincarnation results may vary, as the deities who control such things do occasionally misinterpret words and phrases due to language and cultural differences between Earth and the celestial realms (or just plain carelessness). See Chapter 2 for additional details.

As a final word of warning, while avoiding death of any kind is, of course, highly recommended, you should especially make a point of avoiding a particularly strange or embarrassing death. While deaths of that type actually do tend to attract the attention of the fantasyverse, they also have a much higher chance of causing you to reincarnate into an especially bizarre form. So, unless the idea of living out your second life as a vending machine, pool of water, or jockstrap appeals to you, be extra careful in any sort of odd situations, no matter how safe they initially appear. As a general rule of thumb, if your method of death would make people laugh, or at least roll their eyes at the sheer stupidity of it, it will most likely have a strange and undesired effect on your next life as well.

≋ 2 ≋

Be Prepared

Now that it's only a matter of time before your trip to the fantasyverse, you should prepare yourself both physically and mentally for what's ahead. While everyone enjoys watching a confused, unskilled weakling endure trials and hardships until he grows into a strong and reliable hero, the process isn't nearly as much fun when you're the one living through it. Better to hit the ground running and skip those awkward early stages entirely. The following steps will ensure that you're as prepared as possible for whatever the fantasyverse might throw at you.

Is Your Body Ready?

Physical training takes time, so it's best to start on that as soon as possible. Join a gym, take up a sport, or buy the latest copy of *Dance Fit Adventurelution*. Whatever exercise method you choose, set a routine and stick to it. If you need guidance, our research suggests that doing 100 push-ups, 100 sit-ups, 100 squats, and running 10 km every day has the potential to make you incredibly powerful, though it comes with the risk of losing your hair and becoming so strong that all of your battles are boring. However, keep in mind that you're not necessarily aiming for bulging biceps and a rock-hard six-pack. In a typical fantasy world, you'll need to spend a lot of time hiking, climbing, and running, along with some quick footwork for use in battle. As such, you'll be best served by a moderate amount of strength combined with better than average speed and agility, and as much stamina as possible.

Ideally, you should also include some type of combat training in your exercise routine, as the majority of summoned heroes end up taking on melee roles in battle, and even magic users will find themselves occasionally bereft of their spells in dangerous situations. Guns are unreliable in most fantasy worlds (if they even exist in the first place), but you can't go wrong with traditional weapons such as swords, spears, staves, and bows. Martial arts are another good choice, as you'll never have to fear losing your weapon. Aim for a balanced style with a large variety of blocks and strikes, rather than a style focused on grabs and takedowns such as judo, which may not work well against non-human opponents. Boxing and street fighting can be effective, but much of the fantasyverse has a clear, yet unexplained bias for Asian styles of unarmed combat, so various forms of karate (such as Shorin Ryu) and kung-fu are usually your best options.

If you're aiming for a video game world, you can likely disregard real exercise entirely and focus solely on powering up your avatar. But, just in case you do end up being physically transported to the game world in your own body (an uncommon, though not unheard-of, situation), it's far better to strike a balance between working out yourself, and power-leveling in-game.

When creating your avatar character, we recommend one with the same gender and build as you have in real life. While not strictly required, this will help you avoid an awkward transition period early on as your brain struggles to adjust to a body with a drastically different center of balance; not to mention some very distracting changes to your anatomy. You should also choose a class that allows for a good solo build, as you can't always count on having a full team handy to prevent your glass cannon mage from getting eaten by a giant toad after running out of MP. Conventional melee fighters, well balanced mages, stealthy rogues, and jack-of-all-trades builds are all solid choices depending on your personality and physical prowess. Unconventional builds (such as focusing solely on maxing out your defense in order to gain near invincibility) are worth investigating as well, but only if the end result is truly overpowered and won't result in a giant toad situation. Beyond that, focus on maxing out your character's level and stats as much as possible, and stockpiling powerful items and equipment of all types. Healing items and spells are especially valuable, as are gold, gems, and any other type of universal currency. You can never be too prepared. If nothing else, extra items and gear can be used to better outfit your future party members (see Chapter 9).

Be a Know-It-All

In addition to training your body, you should also train your mind. Note that, in this case, we're not referring to staying in school, studying hard, and getting good grades—though that is a good idea in general, especially if your career goal of being a hero in a fantasy world falls through and you need a backup plan. While a moderate amount of intelligence and basic knowledge is essential for any would-be hero, thriving in a fantasy world requires more specialized knowledge.

Survival skills are a good place to start. While taking time to learn which plants are safe to eat is a bit of a gamble, as fantasy worlds often feature their own unique flora, more general skills such as how to start a fire, build a shelter, find water, and hunt are likely to come in handy at least once during your adventures, if not on a daily basis.

As long as we're discussing boring practical skills, these days many summoned heroes are called upon not just to defeat evil, but to build or rebuild an entire kingdom as well (see Chapter 15). To prepare for that eventuality, studying up a bit on government, organization, project management, and even urban planning can come in handy. You're also sure to find a use for the power of SCIENCE! whether you're using it to wow the natives, give yourself (and/or your kingdom) an edge in battle, or just obtain some of the comforts of home (plumbing, for example). If all this seems like a bit much for you to learn, there may be ways to ensure you have access to such knowledge without having to memorize it all on your own (see the section on survival packs for more details).

Genre-Savviness and You

If you lack the time and/or mental capacity to learn everything, the most important set of knowledge and skills you can obtain by far is genre-savviness. Fantasy worlds, especially those that summon heroes from Earth, tend to operate on a large number of common tropes. By learning to recognize them, you'll be able to immediately predict things, like which of your companions is most likely to mentor you (the oldest one, usually with a beard of some sort), betray you (depending on the type of fantasy world, either the obviously suspicious one, or the one you'd absolutely never suspect), or sleep with you (see Chapter 14). Getting those mixed up can lead to rather uncomfortable situations, to say the least. You'll also learn how to quickly identify the traitor in any government or organization (helpful hint: it's always the second in command), where to find the most powerful equipment (the most inaccessible spot in the entire world), and the best time and method to unlock your hidden power (generally by self-realization, or sheer determination at the most dramatic moment of an important fight). You can also familiarize yourself with a wide variety of fantasy worlds, fantastic beasts, combat styles, and magic systems, which should drastically reduce your learning curve upon arrival. The best way to accomplish this is to immerse yourself in fantasy stories, whether in books, films, or video games. Naturally, you should particularly focus on stories which involve people from Earth being summoned to, or reborn into a fantasy world, as they will likely feature a number of similarities to your own eventual situation (many fantasy worlds aren't known for their high degree of originality). The more you know, the better you'll be able to avoid the common mistakes and pitfalls that typically plague summoned heroes. To help you in this task, we've prepared a list of recommended stories at the end of this book.

You Can Bring It with You ... Maybe

Except in the case of reincarnation, the majority of people who end up in a fantasy world arrive in their own bodies (or that of their avatar, in the case of game worlds). Because of this, they're usually able to keep whatever clothing and other items they have on them at the time. You can take advantage of this trend by going about your daily life wearing strong, comfortable clothing and shoes that are appropriate for many types of weather and terrain. Blue jeans, t-shirts, a jacket, and sneakers are always a reasonable choice, as are track suits. Despite their popularity among female heroes, Japanese schoolgirl uniforms aren't recommended, as the requisite short to mid-length skirt will typically result in cold legs and lots of unintentional fanservice. For that matter, skirts in general (and kilts) are not recommended, as you'll likely find yourself spending long hours hiking, climbing, and fighting. The same applies to any sort of high heels, unless you're deliberately trying to make things more difficult for yourself (if so, remember that bragging rights usually aren't worth the risk of death and twisted ankles). If you want to go the extra mile, wear a swimsuit under your clothes. Aside from providing some extra modesty if you insist on wearing a skirt, you'll also be able to avoid any embarrassing situations when you encounter the inevitable bath house or hot spring (this applies to both male and female heroes).

But clothing is only the start. Anything you can reasonably carry on your body is fair game. A well-prepared future hero should put together a fantasy world survival pack (ideally a sturdy backpack or the like) and keep it on his or her person at all times, even when bathing and sleeping. You might feel a little ridiculous, but it'll all be worth it if you suddenly find yourself whisked away to a fantasy world while in the middle of a shower. Your survival pack should include as many of the following items as possible.

No matter how cute it looks, wearing a short skirt in a fantasy world is sure to result in a combination of embarrassment and windchill.

So You've Landed in a Fantasy World

Fantasy World Survival Pack Checklist

- An Extra Set of Clothes
  - To serve as insurance in case of a poorly timed summoning or battle-induced costume damage; you probably don't want to be known as "the streaking swordsman." (And if you do, please don't tell anyone that you got the idea from this book.)
- A Copy of This Guidebook
  - Or, for that matter, the entire series of *So You've* guides, just in case.
- Emergency Rations
  - In case the local cuisine takes some getting used to, or one of your party members ends up being the cliché cute girl/guy who can't even boil water without turning it into some sort of deadly slop.
- Chocolate, Candy, or Other Snacks
  - There's no better way to make fast friends with a cute girl, monster, or monster girl, than a chocolate bar.
- A Portable Water Purifier
  - Unless you enjoy indigestion.
- Your Weapon of Choice
  - Depending on the size of said weapon and local laws, this may not be possible. But if you can get away with it, do so.
- A Good Flashlight, Ideally with Rechargeable Batteries
  - More reliable than a torch, and far less likely to accidentally set you, your friends, your equipment, or the entire dungeon on fire.
- A Cell Phone or Tablet (the more rugged and waterproof the better)
  - You probably won't get any reception, but you can preload a lot of useful offline apps and files including:
    - eBooks
      - Focus on practical texts and guides on topics such as wilderness survival, leadership, battle tactics, cooking, science, and engineering, along with the entire series of *So You've* guides (just in case something happens to your physical copies).
    - Music
      - You'll probably get bored of the local ballads and harvest

songs. Plus loud, angry music such as death metal can be good for scaring away weaker enemies.

- Photos and Videos of Earth
  - Useful for wowing the locals, or convincing them that you can trap peoples' souls inside the phone. Alternately, media of the more adult variety is perfect for both distracting guards and for getting yourself smacked in the face by your female party members.

- A Portable Video Game System
  - To kill time on rainy days and during long boat rides.
- A Solar Battery Charger
  - Fantasy worlds generally don't feature electrical outlets to recharge your phone and game system.
- Your Favorite Stuffed Animal or Similar Toy
  - At best, it will come to life and fight alongside you. At worst, you'll have something to cuddle at night during the early days of your adventure before you've built up a harem (see Chapter 14).
- As Many Gold Coins as You Can Carry
  - It's the universal currency; weight and purity matter much more than design.
- A Tank
  - To be fair, a good tank won't fit in a bag, and isn't something that most of us can easily get our hands on. But, if you can somehow manage to bring one with you, it's sure to make your journey considerably easier.

In certain circumstances, especially when traveling by portal, you may even be able to bring a companion along for the ride. It doesn't always work, and timing is everything, so cross your fingers and try and keep your chosen partner by your side as much as possible. If you're not sure who to bring, we recommend one of the following.

- Your Dog
  - It's loyal, it can fight, it can scout, it can track, and it's significantly less likely to get kidnapped than any of your other options. Plus, you can pet and cuddle your very good boy or girl whenever you want! However, if your dog is small, cowardly, and/or lazy, you're probably better off choosing a different companion.

- Your Best Friend
  - A fun and trustworthy companion on any adventure. But keep in mind that if you're separated during transit, or shortly after arrival, he or she will likely disappear for a considerable length of time, only to suddenly turn up as one of the enemy's best warriors. This is especially likely if the two of you share any sort of rivalry.
- Your Boyfriend/Girlfriend
  - The companionship and other benefits are always welcome, but be aware that there's a roughly 50 percent chance that one of you will be kidnapped early on and spend several days, weeks, or even months locked up while waiting for your significant other to swoop in for the rescue. You'll also be missing out on the chance to form a new romantic relationship with one (or several) of your traveling companions, so be sure to weigh the risks and rewards of this choice before committing.
- Your Brother/Sister
  - Siblings typically end up serving in more or less the same capacity as a best friend or romantic partner (minus any actual romance; fantasy worlds don't really go for that) with similar odds of getting separated or captured. But, being your sibling, he or she will likely be far more annoying and insufferable about the entire thing.
- Your Mom
  - No, seriously. Sure, it'll be really awkward, but she's probably far more powerful than you can imagine, and will always make sure you've got a hot meal and clean underwear. Just remember, she's doing it all because she loves you so try not to be too upset if she steals some of your limelight.

Choosing Your Boon

While many future heroes make their way to a fantasy world via their own devices or with the aid of a summoner, others are chosen by the gods themselves and sent to aid a world that finds itself in particularly dire straits (such as being overrun by an unstoppable demon king, or lacking any good pizza parlors). In these situations, the goddess

Moms, the greatest and most loving heroes in the fantasyverse.

(due to union rules, all summoned heroes are entitled to be met by a beautiful goddess) will typically grant you a special skill or item to aid in your quest. In most cases, you'll be allowed to choose between anywhere from three to several dozen different options. Unfortunately, due to heavenly budget cuts, summoned heroes are typically limited to one boon each. On top of that, all boons are NOT created equal, so this isn't a choice to make lightly. It can often mean the difference between a fun, enjoyable adventure, and a difficult and dangerous slog, so it's worth taking your time to review the options ... unless it's not. In some cases, you'll be racing the clock. Perhaps you're not the only one who was summoned, and you need to lock down the boon you want before someone else grabs it. Perhaps your body can only exist in the celestial realm for a short period of time. Or, perhaps the goddess will just get bored and decide to kick you out whether or not you've made your decision. Be sure to check with your goddess to find out if one of these situations applies. If so, take a quick glance and just grab the most powerful looking item or ability you see (using the advice later in this section as a guide), as any other approach will likely result in you getting stuck with the short end of the stick.

If time isn't an issue, start by grilling your goddess for as much information as possible about the world you'll be going to, and what threats you can expect to face there. Then, carefully look through the entire list of boons and make note of the ones that seem to be an especially good choice, given the information you've received and your own personality and style. Once you've narrowed your options down to a short list, keep whittling away at it until you've made your final choice. The following are some of the more commonly available boons you may be able to choose from.

- Legendary/Blessed/Cursed Weapons
  - Starting out your adventure with what is essentially an end-game weapon will allow you to easily dispatch any monsters or evil minions you encounter early on. Though, over time, your weapon's power will become less impressive as you face stronger and stronger foes. If you do decide to take a weapon as your boon, try to get one that you're at least somewhat proficient with (an all-powerful bow is worthless if you can't hit the broad side of a dragon), and that can ideally target the big bad's weakness (i.e., a silver weapon if you need to defeat the werewolf king). Also, keep in mind that, even when received as a boon, weapons can usually be lost or stolen if you're not careful. Finally, while the legendary and blessed monikers are often used interchangeably, "cursed" weapons typically have some sort of notable drawback (extreme bloodlust, crippling bad luck, etc.) so approach them with caution.
- Legendary/Blessed/Cursed Armor
  - Similar to the aforementioned weapons, but focused on keeping you alive rather than defeating the enemy. Which, to be honest, is often the most important consideration. As long as your enemies can't kill you, you can probably defeat them eventually. But, as with weapons, your armor's effectiveness will likely fade over time, and it's also subject to loss or theft. There's also the very serious risk that, no matter how powerful the armor is, it'll look utterly ridiculous, leaving you half

naked, dolled up like a giant mascot character, or some other ridiculous fashion faux pas. In general, if the armor leaves you too embarrassed to be seen in public, it's not worth choosing, no matter how powerful it may be.

- Magical Powers
  - These are incredibly varied, but often result in you instantly gaining a collection of mid-to-high level spells of a certain element (fire, wind, etc.) or class (white magic, illusion magic, etc.). As with legendary weapons, these are likely to allow you to breeze through the early parts of your adventure only to level out later on, around when you would have been able to learn those spells normally. If these are what you want, make sure you pick a set that will work well against your opponents (being the world's greatest ice mage won't help you much against an invasion of frost giants), and that won't lead to a giant toad incident.
- Magical Companions/Familiars
  - If you weren't able to bring a companion from your own world, you might be able to pick one up here. Companions or familiars gained in this way can serve a variety of roles from combat, to support, to just being cute, and range from extremely useful to entirely useless. Make sure to carefully review their full list of skills so you know which is which. If you can, you should also try to get a feel for their personalities, as having a companion that constantly shouts "Hey! Listen!" whenever it sees something interesting will eventually drive you crazy, no matter how useful it is.
- Specialized Skills/Knowledge
  - In case you didn't have time to fully train your body or mind as discussed earlier, you may be able to make up for it by instantly gaining the abilities of a master martial artist, a complete knowledge of alchemy, or some such. Only choose one of these as your boon if it's a skill you completely lack, that is certain to be vital to your quest. No matter how much you want to become a word class novelist or champion hot dog eater, it's probably not going to help you much during a fantasy world adventure.
- Immortality
  - Usually an all-around excellent choice, but it often comes with

19

a lot of fine print that you'll want to carefully review. Be sure you understand what limits and conditions the immortality has, whether or not you can still be injured, how well you can (or can't) heal, etc. Being immortal isn't all that much fun if the villain can simply throw you in a cell until you become too old and feeble to move.

- Everything Else
  - There will likely also be some highly unique skills (the power to fly, potion making, the ability to understand any language, etc.) which are either gained innately, or by wearing some sort of accessory. They tend to be highly situational, but the right one can often make all the difference. Assuming you have enough time and knowledge to sort through these, you'll often find the best boon for your particular world and quest somewhere among them.

Before you fully commit to your choice, you should see if there are any loopholes you can take advantage of. While goddesses are all-powerful immortal beings (that nevertheless don't feel like actually bothering to make the effort to save fantasy worlds on their own), they can be a bit absentminded and not well-versed in legalese, so you can sometimes exploit the wording of their offer to secure yourself multiple boons, or something even better. For example, did she really say that you could only have one boon? If the boons are in a box or on a shelf and the goddess merely said to "take something," why not take the entire box, boons and all? The most exploitable situation is typically when a careless goddess offers you "any one thing," as that would not only include the box or weapon rack, but also any divine weapons or items the goddess may be carrying, or even the goddess herself, so be sure not to let the situation go to waste.

Though, as a word of warning, while having a beautiful, all-powerful goddess as a traveling companion may sound appealing, many goddesses aren't always as wise and powerful as they first seem, especially after being thrown out of the heavens and into the mortal world. They're also likely to be quite pissed at you for putting them in that situation. Realistically, choosing a goddess as your boon tends to result in either an easy but boring instant win (where the goddess quickly takes care of everything so she can go home), or a significant handicap (where you find yourself stuck with an underpowered, but very angry deity for the entirety of your adventure). And, just in case you think that she might make a good romantic partner, trust us, she's so not into you. Plus, there's a zillion heavenly laws and regulations against that sort of thing anyway. So, even if recruiting the goddess is technically an option, just resist the temptation and choose something else.

As a final note, if all of the goddesses are otherwise occupied and you find yourself forced to deal with a god instead, be very careful. While there are some wonderful gods in the fantasyverse, they never seem to find themselves on reincarnation duty. And while reincarnation goddesses can be careless or airheaded, their male counterparts are, without exception, either highly incompetent, cruelly vindictive, or both. So, if you find yourself facing one, pay close attention, be as polite and respectful as possible, and hope for the best. And, whatever you do, don't flirt. An incompetent god is the only one who might fall for it (and even then, only if you're his type), but they're too inept to actually give you anything useful in return so it would just be a waste of time. Instead, focus on quickly getting reborn before you get screwed over too badly.

⇛ 3 ⇚

You Made It! Now What?

Whether by luck or persistence, summoning or rebirth, portal or science, successfully making your way to a fantasy world is a big step. However, it's really only a footnote in the epic journey you're about to undertake. There are monsters to slay, kingdoms to build, worlds to save, and pizzas to bake! No matter how well prepared you may be, starting a new life in a brand-new world is a challenging and disorienting experience. There's so much to see and do that you can easily find yourself overwhelmed. It's best to start by spending a few minutes calmly taking stock of your situation, and preparing yourself physically and mentally for what comes next.

Who, or What, Are You?

It's not always possible to keep your original body when traveling to the fantasyverse, especially in the case of reincarnation. So, the first order of business is to figure out who, or what, you are. In most cases, a simple visual examination will suffice. Chances are, you'll be in your normal body along with whatever clothes you were wearing at the time you left Earth behind. If you're lucky, your survival pack and companion (if any) will have also come along for the ride. But even if everything looks normal, it's best to run a few tests. Pat yourself down, run back and forth, do a few jumping jacks. Perhaps your fantasy world has a lower gravitational pull than Earth, granting you super human speed and strength (strangely, the opposite is virtually unheard of). Maybe you'll have spontaneously gained some sort of magical powers. This can also be a good chance to test out your boon, if you got one.

3. You Made It! Now What?

Of course, there's always the chance that, while your mind and spirit made the trip to the fantasyverse, your body got left behind somewhere along the way. If you were aiming for a game world, you may have ended up in the body of your avatar instead. In that case, take a minute to check your equipment and inventory, and test out some of your favorite skills to make sure everything is working the way it does in-game. Do note that, unless you're accustomed to highly realistic VR games, physically performing special attacks or spells in real life is likely a bit trickier than it looks on screen, even with a high-level avatar.

If you're still human, but end up in an unfamiliar body, it's even more vital to take some time to assess not only your appearance, but your physical capabilities as well. Generally, you'll simply be a younger and healthier version of yourself, as a sort of gift from your goddess or the fantasyverse in general. After all, no one really expects an overweight, middle-aged man or hospital-bound girl to travel all over the world and save the day without some sort of improvement to their physical capabilities. But be careful. While some fantasy worlds handwave it as a favor to their summoned heroes, more realistic ones will often subject you to an awkward learning curve as your brain struggles to adjust to your new height and bodyweight. Expect a lot of awkward flailing and painful falls early on. Ideally, you should do you best to overcome this before you encounter any of the locals.

In extreme cases, you may even end up as a baby and have to start over from the very beginning. On one hand, learning to walk, talk, and get through the day without a stack of diapers all over again is not fun. But on the bright side, once you do get past that initial awkward phase, you can easily use your knowledge and skills to be hailed as a child prodigy and go on to shock the world by inventing paper or hair ornaments or something. So relax and enjoy the coddling and diapers while you can.

Since gender swapping is also somewhat common in these situations, you should take a quick look to ensure that you do, or don't, have all the parts that you're used to. A gender swap can be quite distracting for a number of reasons so, once again, it's best to work out the basic functions of your new body before you run into any dangerous or embarrassing situations. Also, be prepared for how people's perception of you may change compared to what you're used to, and try to work it to your advantage when possible. Above all, try not to get too carried away with your new form and stay on task, or you might find yourself requiring a much different, and considerably less family friendly, guidebook.

In very rare situations, there's a chance that you'll find yourself reborn into the body of a familiar character from your favorite fantasy novel, game, or TV show. Unless you want to creep yourself out, try not to think too much about the whole body-swapping thing, and what happened to the character's original mind and personality. Usually, you'll have all of his or her memories in addition to your own. Or, failing at that, you can at least make use of your no doubt extensive knowledge of said character to ensure that no one around you notices the switch. In cases like these, you'll never end up as the original story's hero or main character. Instead, you'll be placed in the body of some side character or minor villain, with the goal of using your familiarity with the source material to change his or her life for the better. Or maybe you'll be Yamcha. (In which case, we are truly sorry for you.) Regardless, while the specifics vary depending on the character, becoming successful in your new life generally just boils down to some combination of "train harder" and "don't be evil."

There's also a very real possibility that you may no longer be human at all. If you find yourself in the body of a humanoid or demi-human race such as elves or beastkin, the adjustment probably won't be especially difficult. In fact, you may find yourself with a host of welcome improvements such as enhanced balance, night vision, increased longevity, or a fluffy tail. However, when the fantasyverse decides to give you such a drastic makeover, it often jumps right to extremes, and you may very well find yourself transformed into an animal or monster. In such cases, expect a far greater learning curve as you struggle to adjust to your new form and get a handle on what you can and can't do. If possible, it's recommended to take a few days or more to really get a feel for things before progressing with your adventure.

A few good questions to ask yourself in this situation include:

- Do all five of your senses work as expected?
- Can you move under your own power?
- Can you talk, or otherwise communicate with the locals?
- Do you need to eat, or otherwise absorb energy and nutrients? If so, how?
- If you're a monster, are you big and scary, cute and collectable, or somewhere in-between?

- Does your new form come with any notable powers or abilities?
- And, perhaps most importantly, how edible does the local wildlife consider you to be?

But what if, upon arrival, you find yourself unable to see? While that certainly makes matters more complicated, don't panic yet. You might be in a dark cave or dungeon. Maybe you have a garbage can on your head. If worst comes to worst and you find yourself completely and fully lacking the sense of sight (either due to sudden blindness or a lack of eyes), then you can panic. But even in such extreme situations, it's best not to get too worked up. While the situation will likely make the earliest parts of your adventure a bit more difficult, in fantasy worlds the hero is never truly blind for any significant length of time. It won't be long before you either find some way to restore your sight, or gain an equivalent ability, such as sensing your surroundings via magic, chi, or some other convenient plot device, so just be careful and make the best of it until then.

Finally, if you're one of the rare few that's unfortunate enough to end up reincarnated as a truly inanimate object, don't worry too much.

Sure, it may not be the reincarnated form that you wanted, but just wait until you unlock Stir Frying Rank 10.

You're guaranteed to be something that you have a deep familiarity with and personal connection to (like soda machines or underwear), and you'll likely be able to gain EXP in order to upgrade yourself and add additional functionality. Beyond that, sooner or later, you're bound to encounter a helpful adventurer who will decide that you, whatever you are, are exactly what she (for "reasons," the adventurer in question will always be female) needs to aid her on her quest. Sure, it may not be quite the fantasy world adventure you were dreaming of, but you can still enjoy a fun and exciting life with your new owner. See the section on supporting characters in Chapter 5 for more information.

Where in the Fantasyverse Are You?

Once you've got the "who" worked out, it's time to focus on the "where." If all went according to plan, you should be in a fantasy world of some kind, as opposed to an alien planet, post-apocalyptic future, prison dimension, or one of the many other locations where inhabitants of Earth occasionally end up. If you do believe that you've somehow missed the fantasyverse and made your way to a different type of world, please set this book aside and locate the appropriate *So You've* guide for your current setting (as previously mentioned, it's always a good idea to keep the entire set on hand, just in case).

Assuming, however, that you have successfully arrived in a true fantasy world, there's still more you need to know. There are a wide variety of fantasy worlds to which you may have been sent. While no two fantasy worlds are exactly alike, the ones that tend to recruit heroes from Earth mostly fall within four classifications, each of which requires different things from its would-be heroes. For now, we'll settle for identifying the type of world in which you've found yourself. More detailed information on how to survive and thrive in each setting can be found later in this book. The four most common world types are as follows:

Standard Fantasy World

Standard fantasy worlds are the sort of pleasantly generic fantasy worlds we all know, love, and are rather bored with. Expect lots of ancient forests, towering mountains, idyllic farming villages, and bustling medieval cities (often with a large castle in the middle). They tend to be inhabited by a combination of humans and other classic fantasy races such as elves (tall with pointy ears), dwarves (not tall with beards), and cat girls (cute with tails). Similarly, you'll also find a collection of staple fantasy monsters like goblins (weak and annoying), dragons (big and deadly), and slimes (small and squishy). Magic will likely be of the standard elemental variety, and operate off a clear and well-defined set of rules and restrictions. That said, don't be surprised if there's a few oddball pieces of advanced technology or some such sprinkled about as remnants of a lost ancient civilization.

Do note that there may be some slight variations in the look and feel of the world and its inhabitants depending on whether it was modeled after medieval Europe (the most common by far), feudal Japan or China, or the equivalent time period from another country on Earth (unusual, but not entirely unheard of). You might even find yourself in a rare past version of Earth where magic and monsters have yet to fade into myths and legends. No one is quite sure why so many fantasy worlds turn to Earth for their inspiration in regard to flora, fauna, architecture, and general civilization, but the most common theories revolve around some combination of human nature, lack of originality, and budget cuts.

You can expect your adventures in standard fantasy worlds to be long epic affairs which will involve traversing much of the known world in search of the ancient spells, relics, and other McGuffins that prophecy says are needed to seal or defeat the current dark lord, dragon lord, or other ancient evil force that's currently threatening the land. There might also be a bit of kingdom building (see Chapter 15) thrown in for good measure.

If the place where you arrive just screams "medieval fantasy," without any particularly unusual elements or events, you're most likely in a standard fantasy world and should assume so unless proven otherwise.

Comic Fantasy World

Comic fantasy worlds are often, for all intents and purposes, very similar to standard fantasy worlds. You can expect to see plenty of forests, mountains, and medieval towns and villages, while interacting with all the usual fantasy races and monsters. Most of them will stick extremely close to their classic clichés and tropes, often to the point of ridiculousness. Others, however, may be modified purely for comedic effect. For example, don't be surprised if the dreaded hellhound, Cerberus, legendary guardian of the gates to the underworld, is a tiny three-headed chihuahua; or if mermaids bear a much stronger resemblance to dugongs or chain-smoking grannies than shell-clad sea nymphs. Expect the internal logic and physics in worlds of this type to be somewhat loose, operating more on the Rule of Comedy and Rule of Cool than science or logic. Magic will likely be much the same way, and will generally be relatively easy to learn and wield as a result.

If you find yourself in a comic fantasy world, you can still expect an epic adventure with lots of traveling, fighting, and McGuffin collecting. But you should also expect quite a lot of comic mishaps, eye-rolling events, extreme clichés (your genre-savviness studies will serve you well here), very bad puns, and fanservice (or possibly its much less pleasant cousin, fan disservice). While the inhabitants of these worlds tend to merely roll with the punches, many summoned heroes get a bit exasperated by it all over time, as they tend to feel like the lone straight man in a world of bad comedians. On the bright side, comic fantasy worlds are among the safest in the fantasyverse as hardly anyone, other than the major villains, ever truly dies (though there are notable exceptions, especially at suitably dramatic times, so keep your guard up). You can, however, expect to be frequently punched, hammered, fireballed, and otherwise beaten in humorous, though strangely not life-threatening ways, often due to no actual fault of your own. Violent misunderstandings are simply par for the course, especially if you're male.

Figuring out whether you've arrived in a comic fantasy world is actually quite simple as they are entirely incapable of letting newly summoned heroes go for more than five minutes (or often 30 seconds) without being the subject of some ridiculous and/or embarrassing situation. If, upon your arrival, you find yourself facing off against extremely idiotic bandits, encountering someone bathing, or crashing face first into either a plate of food or a member of the opposite sex, you can safely surmise that you're in a comic fantasy world.

Video Game Fantasy World

Video game fantasy worlds have become increasingly popular in recent years, as the fantasyverse frequently uses the popularity of gaming to recruit numerous heroes, or players, from Earth. In many ways, they tend to resemble either standard, comic, or even dark fantasy worlds, but with the addition of video game mechanics and elements. It is, however, important to note that worlds of this type come in several notably different varieties.

- True Video Game World
  - In this case, you will literally be inside a video game (either in your normal body or that of your avatar). Everything will operate according to game logic and structure. You will have access to standard game systems and conventions such as menus and status screens, and have to manage your HP, MP, EXP, LVL, and a number of additional abbreviations that you're hopefully familiar with. Any characters beyond yourself and other players will be NPCs operating off AI that, no matter how advanced it may be, won't be on the same level as that of a real person. You may even be able to exploit the AI or other programming elements to your advantage. Do note that, in worlds of this type, your real body will normally remain on Earth, and will need to be cared for during any extended absence.
- Video Game-Style World
  - While a world of this type is based on an actual game (most likely the one you were playing before you arrived), it's a real living, breathing world, rather than a virtual reality recreation. The world will still operate primarily on game mechanics, but you can expect some real-life elements (such as proper physics and bodily concerns) to manifest as well. Anyone you meet will be just as real as you are, and should be treated as such if you want to avoid some very awkward situations (such as explaining to someone why you're stealing a sword out of his sock drawer). As you're in a real place instead of a computer, you may not have access to menus and other in-game conveniences. You're also more likely to get hurt or permanently killed compared to a digital world.
- World with Game Elements
  - Not a true game world, but a different type of fantasy world (probably normal or comic) that has borrowed a few game mechanics. You can expect to gain EXP, level up, and allocate your skill points like in a normal video game. The rest of the world, however, will operate in a much more realistic fashion,

so try not to think of it as a game world. If you do, you may end
up collapsing under the weight of 99 of every item, or getting
stabbed to death while trying to open a non-existent menu.

If you were transported to a fantasy world while playing a video
or computer game, you are almost certainly in a game world of some
type. In fact, it's almost impossible to reach a true video game world or
a video game-style world in any other way. Standard, comic, and dark
fantasy worlds with game elements, however, are becoming increasingly
common in the fantasyverse as a way to quickly acclimate summoned
heroes, and are far less picky about how they're accessed.

Your adventures in a game world are still likely to be big and epic,
but will stick to a more game-like style of progression. You can expect to
find lots and lots of formal quests to undertake, which may range from
solving puzzles, to wiping out seemingly endless hordes of monsters, to
collecting large quantities of items which are inevitably much rarer than
they should be (for example, only expect about one in every ten rats you
kill to actually have a tail; and don't even think about what the guy who
hired you is going to do with all those rat tails once you do find them). Of
course, there will be big important quests related to saving the world as
well, but they'll appear infrequently between bouts of collecting rat tails
(and lizard tails, and wolf tails, and lion tails, and dragon tails, and any
other tails you can think of). You'll also find yourself encountering far
more monsters than you would in any other type of fantasy world (how
else are you going to kill enough kobolds to get fifteen of their tails [or
whatever it is that kobolds have; candles, maybe?]), so be prepared to
spend much of your time fighting for your life. On the plus side, revival
magic and other ways to cheat death are often present, or even common,
so you don't need to worry too much about being overwhelmed by all
those rats and kobolds looking to avenge their lost tails. Unless it's one
of the increasingly common games where a digital death kills you in the
real world as well, in which case you better master the battle system very
quickly before your life is brought to a sudden end by a wild boar or large
flower.

Video game worlds, of any type, are very easy to identify. Keep an
eye out for floating HP gauges, giant green exclamation marks over people's heads, or random passersby talking about going up to level 10 after
collecting their sixtieth giant cobra tail. If you encounter any of those,
you can rest assured that you're in some type of game world.

Dark Fantasy World

Fortunately, people from Earth are rarely summoned to dark fantasy worlds. Unfortunately, rarely isn't the same as never. They're often similar to standard fantasy worlds in terms of their geography and inhabitants, but expect everything to look particularly dark and dreary. At the extreme end, this could mean a world of eternal night filled with crumbling ruins, poisonous bogs, and forests made up of twisted and

Welcome to the dark side of the fantasyverse, where you can rest assured that EVERYTHING wants you dead.

rotting trees. At best, expect things to look rundown, seedy, and dangerous no matter where you go. Unfortunately, dark fantasy worlds are just as miserable and dangerous as they look, if not more so. You can "safely" expect that everyone, from the cannibalistic plague rats, to the poor downtrodden villagers, to the gods themselves are out to rob you, kill you, or worse.

Your standard residents of these cursed worlds are either miserable peasants struggling to eke out a living that a death row inmate wouldn't envy, or cruel and sadistic villains who live (and quickly die) by the overly large sword, bow, whip, spear, or whatever other painful weapon you can think of. Truly good people (Praise the Sun!) are so rare that they might as well be the stuff of myths and, if you do happen to encounter one, you can expect him or her to die a painful death shortly thereafter, just to hammer in how awful the world is. Even the supposed heroes, despite all the goblins they kill, are nothing more than unstable anti-heroes, often only slightly better than the villains.

Any adventures you have will likely result in conflict against a number of extremely powerful and sadistic villains, culminating in a battle against the gods or devils who created the entire twisted system. That is, of course, assuming you survive long enough, which you probably won't. And even if you do, against all odds, manage to triumph against your foes, the entire experience will leave you broken both physically and mentally, turning you into every bit as much of a monster as they were.

In general, dark fantasy worlds can be quickly recognized by their crumbling architecture and depressing atmospheres. You're also almost certain to witness a gruesome murder (quite possibly your own) within minutes of arriving. However, some will disguise themselves as more ordinary fantasy worlds in an attempt to catch you off-guard and make the eventual violent murders, or mind-breaking torture even worse. Worlds such as these are exceptionally dangerous, even by dark fantasy standards. If you're lucky, the world will over-compensate for its inner darkness, resulting in a place that's so insanely bright, colorful, and sickeningly cute that it couldn't possibly be normal. More clever worlds, however, will hide their true nature from you for hours, days, or even weeks before revealing it in the worst manner possible. Fortunately, even the best disguised dark fantasy worlds have cracks in their facades if you know where to look. Keep a close watch for anything that appears more violent or savage than it should, given the rest of the world, along with any particularly disturbing elements of daily life, even if they're only rumors. Such things are almost always signs of a dark fantasy world waiting to pounce.

If the fantasyverse hates you enough to dump you in one of those hellholes, quickly skip to Chapter 13 for some tips to help you stay alive, at least for a short time, and then Chapter 18 for ways that you might be able to escape back to Earth.

Finally, it's worth noting that, while most fantasy worlds fall neatly into one of these four categories, or at least somewhere in between, there is the rare Wonderland or other non-standard world filled with drugged out caterpillars, murderous playing cards, singing orange-haired midgets, and/or water-soluble witches that purposely defy all definition. In such cases, you'll just have to expect the unexpected and figure things out as you go.

⟫ 4 ⟪

First Things First

Now that you've worked out what and where you are, there are still a few things you should take care of before your adventure gets fully underway. Sometimes, you may be thrust into things almost immediately with no time to prepare. But many summoned heroes find themselves with anywhere from a few hours to a few days to become acclimated to their surroundings before encountering anything more serious than an introductory battle. Taking care of these items before your first formal quest or adventure will speed things up, and give your future companions a better impression of your skills and intelligence. You'll find information on the most critical and basic elements here, with more in-depth information about topics such as combat, magic, and equipment in the following chapters.

Are You Insanely OP?

For many, traveling to, and adventuring in, a fantasy world is a form of wish fulfillment. So, there are times when the fantasyverse takes that to the next level and not only brings you to the world of your dreams, but makes you insanely overpowered (OP) as well. One-shotting massive armies? Smacking down the forces of heaven and hell? Shrugging off a nuclear explosion without using a refrigerator? Slipping free from the bounds of time and space? All just another day in the life of an overpowered fantasy world hero.

If you're traveling to a video game world, you may be able to intentionally invoke this by maxing out your avatar's level, stats, and equipment ahead of time (though it will depend a bit on the game balance and whether or not any other similarly powered up players made the trip). Regardless, you're most likely to end up as an OP god among men (or

An endless horde of undead abominations? For an OP hero, that's barely even a warm-up.

elves, gnomes, and dragons) in a video game or comic fantasy world. Though, in the case of the latter, be prepared to be saddled with some sort of hilariously embarrassing weakness (such as exploding if you eat cake) or personality flaw (like being so cautious that you never leave the starting town). OP heroes are somewhat uncommon in standard fantasy worlds, and the only OP characters in dark fantasy worlds are your enemies, who will be sure to use their insurmountable power to torture you and your companions until you snap and give into your own inner darkness.

Ending up as an insanely OP hero can be quite a lot of fun, though it will also rob most of the challenge and tension from your adventures. Some may find that level of power and invincibility wonderfully freeing. Others may lose their hair and motivation while wishing desperately for a decent challenge. Regardless, be sure to fully test the limits of your powers, and never entirely let your guard down. There's always the chance that you'll take an unexpected knife to the back in the middle of a big speech, be poisoned by one of your party member's failed attempts at cooking, or find that, once you've progressed far enough in your adventure, there's at least a few beings even more overpowered than you are.

Learning the Ropes

If your new world is that of your favorite video game, or you were able to interview a goddess on the way over, you may already be familiar with the current state of the world, the way combat, magic, and character growth are handled, what types of threats you're likely to face, and all those other things that, while often common knowledge to the locals, are going to be complete mysteries to otherworldly heroes such as yourself. Fortunately, the rules of the fantasyverse state that all summoned and reborn heroes will be provided with an appropriate guide or mentor shortly after arrival to help them learn what they need to know in order to start their journey. These guides tend to come in one of three models.

Guides: The Old, the Attractive, and the Useless

- The Wise Old Man
  - Very knowledgeable and helpful. He'll be sure to sacrifice himself to save you from an early threat before he can finish teaching you everything you need to know.
- The Attractive Guy or Girl
  - Always a member of the opposite sex. The male version tends to be either a handsome, gallant knight or a brooding bad boy with a heart of gold. Meanwhile, the female will be either cute and impossibly energetic, or beautiful and mysterious but troubled. Either way, he or she will likely accompany you for the entirety of your adventure (minus any time spent kidnapped by the villain), and will become a possible romantic interest.
- The Useless Cute Thing
  - To be fair, not all cute little creatures who want to join you on your journey are useless. If you're in a world that revolves around monster training, they can quickly become a powerful protector. In all other fantasy worlds, however, they're primarily used for their knowledge, advice, and to throw at hungry enemies when you need to make a quick escape.

Unfortunately, the fantasyverse has a no refund or exchange policy when it comes to guides, so whichever one you get, you're stuck with him, her, or it. Regardless, any of the guides should at least be able to tell you a bit about your new world, teach you how to fight (though, if you're properly prepared, you should know that already), and help you join a guild or other similar organization if needed.

One other basic element you might be worried about is the local language. After all, your high school or university probably didn't offer a course in Fantasy Worldese. Fortunately, the common language in a significant number of fantasy worlds just so happens to be either English or Japanese (generally whichever one you speak most fluently). Numerous fantasy linguists have spent years studying the reason for this strange phenomenon. Some believe that the first humans on such fantasy worlds were actually transplanted from modern day Earth to the distant past to found magical civilizations. Others theorize that it's due to some sort of cross dimensional harmonic resonance. There's also the ever-popular theory that the gods just ran out of good ideas for languages and decided to recycle the ones they already had. Whatever the truth may be, there's a very good chance that, aside from adjusting to the local dialect, you'll have no issues with the language whatsoever.

In cases where your fantasy world does feature its own unique language, you still don't need to worry as your goddess or the summoning ritual itself will typically either give you some sort of magical translation ability, or simply implant the knowledge directly into your memory.* Or, if that was somehow overlooked, your guide or another early acquaintance will be able to take care of it for you instead. The only situation where you would find yourself actually having to learn a new language the old-fashioned way is if you're reborn as a baby, in which case you'll have plenty of time to do so.

Obtaining Starter Equipment

Many would-be heroes find themselves in need of suitable clothing, weapons, armor, local money, and a few other world-specific odds and ends shortly after arrival. This can be averted, or at least partially mitigated, by bringing a survival pack as detailed in Chapter 2, or by loading up your avatar's inventory in the case of a game world. But, if you weren't able to do so, and you didn't receive any starting equipment as a boon or a gift from your summoner, you'll need to set about obtaining some. Your guide, or any guild or other group you end up joining, should be able to help there so it's rarely more than a minor inconvenience, albeit an important one.

Of course, once you've reached the first town or city, you can always purchase gear on your own, assuming you've obtained some of the local currency (or a suitable equivalent, such as gold). Ideally, you should try to purchase some of the same clothing and travel essentials that would have been in your survival pack, along with a suitable weapon and armor that's appropriate for your class and body type. Remember that this is starter equipment, so don't expect anything especially powerful. You're bound to trade it in for newer and better gear multiple times over the course of your journey. Just purchase the strongest gear you can currently afford (leaving at least a little bit of money for emergencies), and you'll be fine (unless you're in a dark fantasy world, in which case you'll

---

* Fantasyverse Surgeon General's Warning: The implantation of language data directly into the brain carries a small risk of overload, followed by going *poof*. That is not a good thing. High luck is recognized as an effective countermeasure.

never be fine). If you want to be cautious, you could even purchase a spare set of gear in case anything happens to your first set. For that matter, if you have the money and inventory space, you might want to consider a third set so you have spares for your spares. A little caution never hurts, and you'll be helping to support the small business and the local economy as a whole. Win-win.

If money is a problem, you can always try selling or trading some of the items you brought with you from Earth. Candy, fancy clothes, and flashy electronic devices are sure to attract buyers, but even more mundane items like soft drinks and photographs can wow the locals enough to bring in some coins. Or, if you really don't have anything to trade, you can try to find a job instead. Ideally, you should be working at the adventure's guild, or similar. However, many summoned heroes get their start washing dishes, waiting tables, or doing construction. You likely won't want to stick with these menial positions for too long, but a few hours, a few days, or even a week or two if necessary, can provide you with all the cash you need to get started on your adventure proper, and may even lead to some useful connections. So don't be afraid to roll up your sleeves and get your hands dirty.

Avoiding an Early Death

If you've determined that you're in a dark fantasy world, please skip to Chapter 13 for a much more detailed explanation of how to hopefully keep yourself alive. For all other fantasy worlds, the survival rate for summoned or reincarnated heroes is quite high, even the ones without insanely overpowered stats and skills. It's quite likely that you'll have met your guide, obtained your starter equipment, and possibly even gotten in some good training before you find yourself in any situation that's even remotely dangerous. However, there is a chance that you'll find yourself in the aforementioned introductory battle shortly after your arrival. Even if that is the case, there's no need to worry. Your first foes will typically be either low-level monsters, or extremely incompetent robbers who you'll be able to defeat even without any particular skills or weapons. Just make use of all that training you did back on Earth. Or, if you've got more flab than abs, just scream and flail your arms around wildly, that's probably good enough. On the off chance that you do run into something stronger than you can handle, you can expect your guide to show up and save you at the last second. Just try your hardest and don't give up. That said, if you really do find yourself outclassed, feel free to turn tail (perhaps literally) and run. And don't forget to scream bloody murder while you're at it. Some guides aren't quite as on the ball as others, but there's nothing like a bit of frantic shrieking to get their attention.

Once you've gotten past that first battle, you're probably safe for a while. Sure, there will be more monsters and other enemies to deal with, but they'll always be something that you and your companions can either defeat or escape from without too much difficulty. You will eventually find yourself navigating perilous terrain and fighting for your life against powerful high-ranking enemies, but all that comes later.

≋ 5 ≋

Rising of an Isekai Hero

Whether you made your way to a fantasy world via rebirth, reincarnation, summoning, or even finding a portal, it's easy to assume that you're the hero who will save the world. And, in most cases, you'd be correct. However, while we really hate to rain on your parade, there is a small chance that you might not actually be the hero. If that turns out to be the case, deviating from your proper role and trying to be the hero anyway is likely to result in a cruel death, or at least an utterly humiliating defeat. And hey, there are actually perks to not being the hero. So, before we move on, let's make sure you're really "the chosen one."

Identifying Your Role

If you came to your new fantasy world on your own, rather than as part of a group, then congratulations! There's a 95 percent chance that you're the hero. However, you may unfortunately be part of the remaining 5 percent if you met and (willingly or unwillingly) teamed up with a troubled hottie just before or after your arrival. As described in Chapter 9, a troubled hottie is a highly attractive but lonely member of the opposite sex, struggling with a great burden of some sort. While they often serve as party members, it's not unheard of for a troubled hottie to be the true hero, leaving you to take on the role of supporting character and chief romantic interest. If you have, in fact, partnered with such an individual, please try not to despair and answer the following questions about your relationship then add up the points in order to determine which of you is, in fact, the hero.

- Did he or she save you from certain death when you first met?
  - ○ Yes +1 (+2 if you were literally swept off your feet).
  - ○ No

The Hero Quiz! Guaranteed to properly identify your role or your money back! (Moneyback guarantee not valid on Earth, the moon, or anywhere in the fantasyverse.)

- Is he or she clearly heroic in appearance, stature, goals, etc.?
  - ○ Yes + 1
  - ○ No
- Is he or she royalty?
  - ○ Yes +1
  - ○ No
- Is he or she a far more powerful fighter than you are?
  - ○ Yes +1
  - ○ No (-1 if considerably weaker).
- Did you swear fealty to him or her? (Note that this does not include promises of friendship or mutual aid.)
  - ○ Yes +2
  - ○ No (-2 if he or she swore to protect or otherwise aid you).
- Are you an inanimate object?
  - ○ Yes +5
  - ○ No

5. *Rising of an Isekai Hero*

Total Relationship Points:

- -3–1: Congratulations, you're the hero! Enjoy your life of adventure.
- 2: Still probably the hero, but you may want to hold off on the business cards for a little while just to make absolutely sure.
- 3–12: You are, unfortunately, not the hero. But you do get to be his or her most trusted companion and eventual love interest, so it's not all bad. Really! We're serious. Don't give up and please read the section on supporting characters later in this chapter for more information.
- 13+: You're either a cheater or really bad at math. Get a calculator (or an abacus) and give it another try.

If you came to your new fantasy world as part of a group of friends, siblings, classmates, gamers, or the like then your role can be considerably harder to identify, especially early in your adventure. But you can use the following questions to form a reasonable guess. Do note that, on occasion, a group may contain more than one hero, or the word hero may be used to refer to all of you as a collective, so don't automatically discount your own claim to the title just because someone else also fits the bill.

- Were you deceived and recruited by a villain shortly after arrival?
  - If so, you're the hero's rival at best. Or, at worst, a petty villain. This is why you shouldn't accept sleigh rides from a stranger, even if she has candy.
- Were you kidnapped shortly after arrival?
  - You're a supporting character and possibly the hero's love interest. Better hope you're put in a comfy cell, because it might be quite a while before said hero actually gets around to rescuing you.
- Did someone specifically single you out as the hero?
  - You're probably the hero. Unless you're a jerk, in which case you'll be upstaged by another member of your group sooner or later. As a note, many jerks lack the self-awareness necessary to identify as such, so you may want to ask the others for their opinions.
- Do you have special knowledge and/or skills that the rest of the group lacks?
  - Once again, as long as you're secure in your non-jerkiness, you're probably the hero.

- Are you the only member of the group who isn't a jerk?
  - You're the hero. Try not to let the others bother you too much, karma will catch up to them eventually.
- Are you clearly the weakest and least useful member of the group?
  - You're probably the hero, though it might take a while for you to uncover and grow into your true potential. Until then, just work hard and do your best to help the others as much as possible. Alternately, if you're in a comic fantasy world, there's a very real chance that, even if you're not officially recognized as the hero, you'll end up saving the day through sheer klutziness and incompetence instead. Or you may just end up as the butt of every single joke.... Though in that case you can at least take solace in knowing that your pain is bringing your friends and allies the third greatest gift they can receive, laughter.
  - Do note that the above does not apply if you're a jerk, or show clear malice and/or jealousy towards the other group members. In those cases, the best you can hope for is to become a petty mid-boss type villain who has his pride (and head) crushed by the real hero. To avoid this fate, simply don't be an asshole (as hard as that might be for some of you).
- Are you a total wuss? And, if so, will you try hard to change?
  - If yes, you're either the hero or one of the more important supporting characters. Keep trying and never give up on yourself. You'll come through when it counts.
  - If no, you're a side character who just hangs around in town and doesn't serve any real purpose. Maybe you can give your life a tiny bit of meaning by running a shop or restaurant or something. After all, everyone like pizzas, or swords, or pizza swords (er, never mind that last one).
- Do none of the above apply?
  - You're a supporting character. Enjoy working just as hard as the hero with none of the accompanying fame or recognition.

Playing the Supporting Character

If you've determined that you're a supporting character, whether in service to a troubled hottie or one of your companions from Earth,

It could be worse. At least you're not that annoying guy who gets killed five minutes into the adventure.

then it's best to contentedly settle into your new role and wholeheartedly support your hero. Not doing so drastically increases your chances of an early death. As a supporting character, there are many different roles you may fill depending on your skills and inclinations. In general, you'll be serving as a member of the hero's party, and helping him or her with all that stuff heroes do such as fighting, protecting the weak, killing monsters, solving puzzles, destroying evil, exploring the world, and slaughtering enemies. You might even end up as one of the hero's potential romantic partners, if you're so inclined. Even if your skills aren't suited to combat, you can always aid the hero in other ways, such as giving advice, telling fortunes, warning of enemy attacks, chopping up vegetables, dismembering monster corpses, jumping in front of a knife or arrow, or just carrying all the bags. Either way, you'll still get the full fantasy world adventure experience from beginning to end (minus any time you spend kidnapped). Even better, if the hero somehow neglected to read this guide before arrival, you can use your extensive knowledge to steer him or her down the proper path to victory.

However, considering that the average hero's party tops out at around half a dozen members, if you were summoned as part of a large group (such as a high school class, or an MMO player base), you might not make the cut. In that situation, you have several possible options. First and foremost, there are two scenarios you want to avoid. One is an early death due to carelessness, arrogance, fear, or stupidity. While the hero will certainly learn and grow from your mistakes, that doesn't really make up for the fact that you were eaten by a giant toad or a killer hippopotamus. The second "bad ending route" is when you let yourself become jealous of the hero's power and popularity. Jealousy leads to anger. Anger leads to hate. And hate leads to a giant bird kicking you in the balls.

Fortunately, there are other options. You could aid the hero from behind the scenes as you go on your own (somewhat less impressive) adventures, fighting monsters and thinning out the forces of evil. There may even be times you get to temporarily join up with the hero's group for major battles. If fighting isn't your thing but you still want to contribute, you could try using your boon and/or Earthly knowledge to help the forces of good by forging powerful weapons, introducing modern farming techniques, or designing battle ready underwear. Finally, if you want to avoid conflict entirely, you could always hang out in a relatively safe area, pleasantly forgotten, and live out a more ordinary fantasy life fishing, raising slimes, or running a restaurant. While it may not be as exciting as facing off against the demon lord, you can still enjoy magic, cat girls, and all the other perks of fantasy life with considerably less risk of death or dismemberment.

A Note for Villains

It's quite common for at least one member of a group summoning to become a villain, more in the case of especially large groups. Maybe you're jealous, afraid, or just really arrogant. Or, perhaps you were always an evil asshole, and this is the first time you can really be your true self. However, while giving into those base urges can be fun or even freeing for a time, it's also a surefire path to a painful defeat and, most likely, death. You might be able to get by as a violent anti-hero, or a morally gray mercenary (so long as you never directly oppose the true hero), but anything worse than that is guaranteed to end in disaster, so do your best to reign in your inner darkness and remain at least tenuously on the side of good.

If you came to the fantasyverse on your own and naturally fell into the role of a villain, that's a different situation entirely, and one where being evil may actually be your best course of action in order to succeed and survive (see our upcoming guide *So You've Decided to Brutally Conquer a Fantasy World*). But remember, that only applies when you're on your own. If anyone else from Earth came along for the ride, you can bet that at least one of them will become a hero and rise up to strike you down. And that's only if karma doesn't decide to literally knock you off a cliff beforehand. Stay good.

≋ 6 ≋

Combat and You

The fantasyverse doesn't pull people from Earth to give them a free vacation. Fantasy worlds have a unique knack for attracting all manner of potentially world-ending disasters; from rampaging monsters to evil empires, to rogue AIs (escapees from sci-fi worlds, apparently), to junk food shortages. And it's inevitably the job of any otherworldly hero or heroes to set things right. Sure, the inhabitants of said worlds could do something about all these crises themselves, but outsourcing is much more economical. And, the most common way to deal with all of these dangerous problems is inevitably to beat the ones responsible into submission. If you were able to learn a bit of armed or unarmed combat back on Earth, it should serve you well in your new life and let you skip much or even all of the initial training that many heroes need to go through at the start of their adventures. Failing at that, you might be able to get combat skills via a boon, or have them mysteriously bestowed upon you early on via a convenient plot device or magical item. Worst comes to worst, you should still be able to pick things up pretty quickly the old-fashioned way via lots of sweat and hard work. (But really, who wants to do that?) While the specifics of combat and battles vary a bit from world to world, the following is some good general advice to help you start kicking ass and taking names (or tails).

Have Some Class

While social graces come in handy if you find yourself rebuilding a kingdom (Chapter 15) or attending a fancy dinner, class has a different meaning when it comes to fantasy worlds. Broadly speaking, heroes and other adventurers each belong to one or more classes which determine their general combat style and skills, from magic wielding sorcerers to spoony bards. The overall structure of the class system, and how formally each class is defined, tends to be most strict in video game worlds and worlds with game elements, but it's present in some form or another in virtually every world in the fantasyverse.

Your starting class may be set prior to your arrival based on your avatar (in the case of video game worlds) or your boon (if you were summoned by a goddess). If not, it will be given to you upon arrival or when you register with a guild. Though, if you lack access to a status menu, you might not have any way to check it early on. While there's a small chance that you'll be stuck with your starting class for the remainder of your adventure, it can normally be changed (formally or informally) via menu options, training, or certain events (completing various challenges, divine blessings, earning enough XP, etc.). Be sure to check with your guide about that. You'll also want to ask whether your new world allows you to multi-class (use all the skills and abilities of two or more classes at the same time), and if you can keep your current skills and stats when switching classes, or if a class change is more akin to starting over from scratch. This will allow you to better plan your development and progress, and save you the hassle and embarrassment of having to save the world while stuck as an idol singer or jolly piper.

There's a near infinite number of classes available to choose from. Some are commonly available on nearly every world in the fantasyverse, while others are exceedingly rare and unusual. The following list covers some of the more useful classes that you're likely to find at your disposal.

- Hero/Adventurer/Freelancer
    - A general, all-purpose class that's good for those who want to be a jack-of-all-trades. While it tends to lack a particular specialty, it makes up for it by allowing the use of a wide variety of weapons, skills, and techniques. Most importantly, having "adventurer" or "hero" as your official title is just plain cool and looks great on business cards.
- Warrior/Swordsman/Spearman/Etc.
    - Melee classes such as these focus on close- to mid-range combat. Depending on the specific class, it might allow for a variety of different weapons, or focus on a particular one. If you do choose to specialize, make sure to pick a weapon that's useful in a wide variety of situations, and won't get you any

The fist is mightier than the sword. At least so long as you properly harness your chi and your opponent has a really crappy sword.

weird looks. Everyone respects a good swordsman or spear-maiden, not so much a rodman, bellboy, or bear-girl.

- Monk/Martial Artist
  - Why rely on a weapon when you can beat down enemies with your bare hands? While the training can be quite harsh, with enough practice, you should not only be able to punch and kick your foes into submission, but also harness your chi to strengthen your abilities, fire energy beams, and make your enemies explode. Do note that, in some worlds, this class might require a whole lot of standing in place and screaming while waiting for your energy to charge. A good throat spray is recommended.
- Archer/Gunner/Sniper
  - These classes are for those who prefer to stand back and defeat their enemies from a safe distance. Depending on who you ask, this is either tactically brilliant or f'ing cheap. While bows are by far the most common long-range weapon in the fantasyverse, a handful of worlds have advanced to the

level where basic firearms are available instead. Be warned, although these classes might seem to be the perfect choice for a more safety-minded hero, they're often lacking when it comes to close combat. As such, learning how to properly scream and run away after using up all of your ammo is a very useful secondary skill.

- Thief
  - While not the most heroic class, thieves have a wide variety of useful skills such as picking locks, detecting traps, sneaking by unnoticed, and stealing underwear. If you choose this as your class, don't be surprised if your party members keep a rather close eye on their wallets.
- Ninja/Assassin
  - Take a thief, add skills in sniping, poisoning, and general combat, and you have an assassin. Toss in some smoke bombs, logs, and throwing stars to get a ninja. Users of these classes

Thieves, always much more fun when they're on your side.

tend to live in the shadows, feared and unknown, so they're not often considered a suitable choice for a hero. But they do have a devoted following, and their ability to remain unseen while wearing bright orange clothes and eating ramen is rather impressive.

- Defender/Tank/Shield Guy
  - A melee class focused on defense, rather than offense. A true master of the shield is near unkillable, and can also protect his or her allies from harm. However, it's not the best choice for solo adventurers, as users of this class can struggle to deal any significant damage to their enemies, and often have to resort to either chipping away at their opponent's health over the course of a long, slow battle, or enlisting the help of raccoon girls and overweight birds to speed things up.
- Magician/Black Mage/Sorcerer
  - Offensive magic users harness the elements to summon fireballs, blades of ice, and really big rocks to crush, stab, burn, and otherwise pulverize their enemies. These classes are usually the top of the list in terms of sheer firepower. However, magic users tend to be severely lacking in physical strength and endurance. Furthermore, in most fantasy worlds, using too much magic in a short time will leave them exhausted and at serious risk of getting stabbed, smashed, or eaten by giant toads. As such, it's a class that works best as part of a balanced party.
- Healer/White Mage/Priest
  - A must-have for any adventuring party, a white mage serves three primary roles. The first is to aid his or her teammates with powerful healing magic that can seal wounds, regrow lost limbs, and possibly even reverse death itself. The second is to destroy undead and demonic monsters with holy power. The third is to get kidnapped and sit around waiting for rescue. Since that last one requires a rescuer, it's not a recommended class for solo adventurers.
- X-Mage
  - Some fantasy worlds feature other types of magic beyond the basic white and black, such as time magic (slowing down and speeding up enemies and allies) and illusion magic (for those days when you just can't get your hair right). While all of these

classes are useful in their own way, and have the rare, super-powered practitioner, they're generally highly situational and most useful as a secondary class rather than your primary focus.

- Magic Swordsman/Spellblade
  - A very popular hybrid class that allows users to infuse their swords with the power of various elemental magic spells. As such, it provides you with the strength and endurance of a melee fighter, and the power and versatility of a black mage. It does, however, require precise training and control to make sure that you don't set yourself on fire along with your sword.
- Paladin
  - Holy warriors blessed by the gods, paladins combine powerful melee techniques with white magic to protect their allies and smite evil. This is an extremely useful class to have when fighting against unholy monsters such as demons and undead. Unfortunately, choosing paladin as your class also gives you a bonus 10 ranks in Self-Righteous Asshole, which can be off-putting for the rest of your party.
- Summoner/Monster Trainer
  - A summoner calls forth beasts and spirits from another dimension, while a monster trainer captures and trains wild monsters. Some fantasy worlds revolve around this class, complete with monster training schools and tournaments. In all others, it's a rare and exotic choice. Either way, you can use your monsters to fight for you, transport you from place to place, and even handle more mundane tasks such as heating food, doing laundry, and charging your cellphone, all while you sit back, safely out of danger, and occasionally yell at them to dodge. See Chapter 8 for more information about choosing and raising your monsters.
- Supporter
  - A catch-all class for non-combatants that otherwise aid the rest of the party, usually by carrying all of their stuff. Unsurprisingly, this is not a class that you actually want to choose for yourself.
- Chef
  - Summoned heroes still need to eat. As such, this can be a useful secondary class if you want to impress your party members during your journey, and it makes for a good career

choice after you've finished saving the world from evil (see Chapter 17). There are also a few recorded instances of worlds with alternate victory conditions (see Chapter 16), where top-notch cooking skills are actually required for success. Finally, while this isn't normally considered a combat class, a good chef's knife skills and knowledge of anatomy can actually be put to deadly use when needed. Besides, werewolf sashimi tastes a lot better than it sounds.

- Bard/Musician/Songstress
  - In some fantasy worlds, music and song are closely tied to magic, and properly trained singers and musicians can use their talents to harness magical energy and cast powerful offensive and defensive spells. Non-magical members of these classes, however, are mostly known for annoying their party members and getting kidnapped. That said, with a bit of creativity, their skills can be turned to combat. A tuba, for example, makes an excellent bludgeoning weapon, while a pipe or flute can become a deadly blowgun. And don't even ask about what you can do with a saxophone.

Skills to Master

The skills available to any summoned or reincarnated fantasy world hero vary wildly depending on your world, class, and even individual characteristics. As such, it's impossible to create any sort of definitive list of must-have skills. Ideally though, you should try to obtain and master the following types of spells or abilities:

- Detection
  - Sure, you can find a trap or an enemy ambush by walking right into it, but actually noticing it beforehand is a lot less painful.
- Appraisal
  - Better to know if the liquid in that vial is a potion, poison, or ogre blood before you drink it.
- Healing
  - Staying alive is generally the best way to avoid dying.
- Powerful Physical Attacks
  - The details don't matter so long as you can effectively smash, stab, eviscerate, or otherwise annihilate your enemies.

54

- Elemental Attacks
  - In general, you want to be able to burn plants and bugs, bury beasts, zap anything liquidy, freeze reptiles, and blow birds (away with wind; what did you think we meant?).
- Long Range Attacks
  - To handle archers, snipers, and monster flies.

Unless you're OP, there's a good chance that you won't be able to obtain every type of skill listed here, so instead try to get party members (see Chapter 9) and magic items that can cover whatever areas you yourself may be lacking. However, when it comes down to it, the skills you should put the most effort into mastering are the ones you have. Even the seemingly useless ones. A little creativity goes a long way. Drop your foes into a pitfall, evade their attacks with your awesome dance moves, cause a wardrobe malfunction and paralyze them with embarrassment, pump them full of gas and flaming soda cans until they explode. The possibilities are endless. You never know when your ability to perform party tricks or dispense racy magazines could save your life.

Gaming the Battle System

As mentioned in the previous section, a bit of creativity goes a long way in the fantasyverse. And, with enough creativity, observation, and genre-savviness, you might be able to find a full-on exploit. While it's only natural for video game worlds to have the occasional bug or glitch that can be taken advantage of, even some fantasy worlds without any game systems can contain very exploitable loopholes in their battle mechanics or other elements, especially if they were created by one of the ditzy goddesses who are usually on reincarnation duty. The exact specifics vary wildly from world to world, but perhaps you could increase your defense so high that you become invincible, or raise your speed to the point where no one else can hit you. Maybe you can eat the monsters you kill to gain their powers, or take advantage of easy resurrection magic to wear enemies down with your infinite supply of extra lives. While tricks and techniques like this don't always exist (dark fantasy worlds in particular tend to be highly resistant to any sort of technique or exploit that would give the hero even a tiny hope of victory), it's worth spending a bit of time thinking and experimenting to see if you can stumble across one, as they can make your life far, far easier.

Notes for Non-Combatants

While your new life will almost certainly involve fighting, there are rare exceptions. Perhaps you're supporting the hero, rather than taking on that role for yourself. Or maybe you're in a world with an alternate victory condition (see Chapter 16). In either case, it's still a good idea to hone some combat skills just in case. You never know when the hero will be incapacitated, or a hungry dragon will decide it doesn't like the pizza you cooked. However, it is quite possible that, if your new world takes its class distinctions very seriously, you may be completely incapable of combat. In such cases, be creative, rely heavily on your party members, and be sure to practice running away. Other useful skills for

Supporting characters, the official pack-mules of the fantasyverse.

non-combatants include: carrying large heavy bags, cutting up defeated monsters for valuable crafting components, and sitting patiently for long periods of time while kidnapped (in the latter case, please also read *So You've Gotten Yourself Kidnapped*). In the end, just train up the skills you have as much as possible, and you'll be fully prepared to cook, build, game, puzzle, or otherwise make your way towards victory.

⇒ 7 ⇐

Magical Me

One of the key elements that makes a fantasy world a fantasy world (as opposed to a plain old, boring medieval world) is the presence of magic. In some parts of the fantasyverse, magic is practically as common as air, infusing itself into every aspect of daily life. In others, it's a rare skill, all but lost, and possessed by only a chosen few. Either way, magic is out there, somewhere, and is sure to play a major role in your new life.

The Rules of Magic

There are countless types of magic, and magic systems spread across the fantasyverse. Some are extremely unusual and unique, such as ingesting various metals and using them as a medium to perform spells, or tying magical abilities to 80s–style dance-offs. However, the type of fantasy worlds that summon heroes from earth are rarely that creative, and their magic tends to fall into one of several clearly defined categories.

- Generic Magic
  - Magic is part of daily life, and standard black and white magic are commonplace. Learning how to wield magical energy and cast spells is supposedly a long and complex process that's nevertheless handwaved at every opportunity. "It's magic, yo!" If you have the potential, all you really need to do is literally wave your hand or wand around while saying some type of simple chant, which generally concludes by yelling out the name of the spell as loudly as you can. Magic can be used to do just about anything you need it to (with, perhaps, a handful of clearly defined exceptions), provided you have enough magical power and can think of a suitably cool/dorky rhyme or chant.

Though there are some worlds that decide to it make it a little harder, requiring the use of certain items or spell forms (often drawn or carved on various surfaces) to cast spells, but even then, there's usually a way around that annoying limitation if you look hard enough.

- Video Game Magic
  - Magic is common, but restricted to certain classes. Forget study or hard work, you can learn new spells by leveling up and/ or spending your skills points on them, though hand-waving and chanting are still likely required. Every spell you cast will consume a set amount of MP, which can typically be restored by resting or drinking a special potion. Magic does, however, tend to be somewhat more restricted in its power compared to other systems, and can only be used to cast a set of clearly defined spells such as healing or blowing everything up.
- Hidden Magic
  - Magic is woven into the fabric of the world, and you'll see its effects in various plants, creatures, and perhaps even items that are used in daily life. However, it's not something that normal people can actually harness or make direct use of, so don't expect to fly on a broomstick or throw any fireballs. If spells can be cast at all, it will only be by lost races, or through the use of ancient artifacts that everyone "conveniently" forgot how to make.

It is also worth noting that, in virtually all fantasy worlds, regardless of the magic system used, there will exist at least a handful of powerful magical relics or artifacts left behind by an ancient civilization (who, despite their advanced knowledge and magical powers, mysteriously disappeared centuries ago). These relics could be as small as a ring, or as large as an entire city. But they can all be counted on to completely ignore any and all rules of magic in order to further the dark lord's plan, or help you counter it. Possibly both. Finding and securing them is bound to be a major part of your adventure.

Are You a Muggle or a Wizard?

In all fantasy worlds, there exists a certain percentage of the population that is completely and utterly unable to use magic in any way, shape, or form. This percentage could be as high as 99 percent, or as low as nobody except you. Unless you received your magic as a boon, or have access to a status screen, it might be difficult to gauge your magical potential upon arrival. Fortunately, any skilled magic user should be able to, at very least, sense your basic potential (or lack thereof) and elemental affinity (if that's a thing). Guilds, spell shops, and magic schools will typically also have some type of device that fulfills the same purpose.

While magical potential is often either innate or tied to specific classes, you may be able to increase it by leveling up, fulfilling certain conditions, or via the use of special artifacts or rituals. Many worlds will also have a selection of magic items you can find or purchase, which will give you access to at least a limited number of spells. Do note, however, that many of these require at least a minimal amount of magical affinity in order to use.

If you have absolutely no magical potential whatsoever, try not to get discouraged. Chances are, you'll eventually gain immense magical powers via a lost artifact or ritual. Or, in some cases, literal deus ex machina. So just do your best without it, and rely on your more magically inclined party members until then. Even if your magical powers never awaken, there's still not much to worry about. Swords (and spears, and bows, and flutes) are just as useful in most situations, and often far quicker and easier to use. When you can jump twenty feet into the air and cut a small mountain in half, magic doesn't seem all that necessary.

Spell Casting for Dummies

As previously explained, casting spells, once you've learned them, is often simply a matter of waving your hands around and saying a suitable phrase or rhyme before yelling out the name of the spell. Simple enough. But here are a couple tips to optimize your technique.

First, while the phrase and spell name might be preset, you may also be able to choose your own. In which case, you should be sure to go with something that sounds suitably cool and impressive. "Here comes Lots of Fireballs!" is a bit lame compared to "Burn my enemies to ash, Rain of Hellfire!" Though, if you're in a comic fantasy world, something silly like "Goodness, gracious, Great Balls of Fire!" might actually work better. Giving praise to the god or gods of your particular world can also be a good choice, especially the more vain and angry ones, as they can be apt to make your spell blow up in your face if you don't. You should, however, avoid phrases that include boasting or bragging, as the fantasyverse loves to punish that sort of behavior. If your phrase is something like "The future queen commands-," you can bet that you won't be the one wearing the crown. Similarly, taunting phrases such as "you'll never survive this" are pretty much guaranteed to cause the opposite effect. Deception, however, is totally fine (if socially frowned upon). Yelling out

Overly long incantations are best suited for poetry slams and literary journals, not actual battle.

"Fireball!" and then dropping a boulder on your opponent's head is a great way to catch him off guard. There's also something to be said for brevity. It doesn't really matter how cool your 20-stanza epic poem is if your opponent stabs you in the gut before you can finish reciting it. Sometimes something short and sweet like "Burn!" or "Wind!" really is the best choice, even if it's not as impressive.

Another thing you should be aware of is your magical power or energy supply. You're probably all familiar with the classic scene where the hero, or villain, is about to finish off his opponent only to realize that he's run out of bullets. While guns are a rarity in the fantasyverse, and running out of arrows is strangely uncommon, mages can easily find themselves in a similar situation. While it depends on the magic system being used, most spells require MP or some other form of energy from the caster. If you run out, no more magic. That can range from mildly embarrassing (and lead to lots of bad jokes about performance anxiety) to deadly if you run out of power in the midst of battle, or while flying, so be sure to always monitor your remaining magic power. Ideally, you should also carry a large stock of magic restoring items (if they exist) so you can quickly recharge as needed.

Spells for Fun and Survival

While it's easy to focus on using magic for combat and healing, it has many other applications that can prove very useful during your adventures. The following are just a few of the more common ones.

- Fire Magic
  - Great for starting campfires, cooking food, finding your way in dark places, and even drying your clothes. You can also incinerate the remains of your enemies to make sure that they're really dead.
- Water Magic
  - Useful for cooking, cleaning, laundry, bathing, and drinking. Plus, nothing shuts up an annoying party member faster than dumping a few buckets worth of water on his head.
- Wind Magic
  - With enough power and control, wind can be used to fly and manipulate the weather. It can also guarantee you the win if you somehow end up in a kite flying competition.

- Earth Magic
  - Build shelters and fortifications! Create golems! Bury trash (and bodies)! Wonder why the heck it's still called Earth magic even when you're not on Earth!
- Lightning Magic
  - A little bit of electricity is great for zapping particularly annoying teammates. It also makes fishing a cinch and provides a quick and easy way to charge your phone.
- Telekinesis
  - Perfect for flight, if you're strong enough. If not, you can still use it for carrying your bags, distracting your enemies, and picking up all those icky monster parts that you need for crafting, but don't really want to touch.
- Time
  - Never be late for a meeting ever again. Give yourself some extra time to sleep in. Fast forward through all the boring parts of your adventure. After all, you've got all the time in the world.
- Illusion
  - No need to fix your hair every morning, just whip up a good

With lightning magic, you've got the power!

63

illusion. Want to spend all day in your PJs? No problem. Go around in comfort while making everyone think that you're wearing your Sunday best. For that matter, why bother with clothes at all?* Just enjoy the breeze and let your magic do all the work.

---

* Fantasyverse Surgeon General's Warning: Illusionary clothing provides no protection against heat, cold, wind, rain, swords, spears, arrows, dragon breath, poison slime, or really anything at all. It has also been known to vanish suddenly due to dispelling effects, lack of mana, or just to embarrass you. Please use with caution.

≡ 8 ≡

Gearing Up

In most fantasy worlds, your equipment is nearly as important as your skills and magic. Good weapons, armor, and accessories serve to increase your offensive and defensive power, while also granting special bonuses and abilities. Meanwhile, consumable items provide healing, magic restoration, quick getaways, and more. And that's only the beginning.

Becoming a Power Shopper

While you're certain to find new items and equipment in the occasional treasure chest, or being carried around by monsters (never mind what a giant two-headed dog is doing with a long sword), the fastest and simplest way to stock up on all necessary weapons and items is by visiting the local shops and merchants. Hopefully you brought enough gold to get started. If not, consider taking on an odd job, or fighting some of the weak monsters who live in the area (the Proper Balance and Pacing Act of 1173 guarantees that newly summoned or reincarnated heroes will always arrive in the part of the world that's home to the weakest monsters), until you've amassed enough of the local currency to afford a decent set of starter equipment.

If you plan on making a home base in your starting town or city, as opposed to leaving it behind to never be seen again as you travel the world, it's worth identifying a favorite shop which you can frequent while building up a good relationship with the owner (generally either a gruff but kindly older man, or a cute and energetic young woman). Doing so will eventually lead to all sorts of special discounts and insider deals. Otherwise, just ask the locals to point you to the best (and likely only) shop for whatever it is you need to obtain.

While it is important to leave yourself enough money for room and board, feel free to invest every additional coin into your equipment. For weapons and armor, aim to buy the strongest (class appropriate) ones that you can afford. A better weapon will allow you to defeat stronger monsters, which inevitably drop more money (don't worry about why the monsters are carrying around bags full of coins) or sellable materials. Meanwhile, better armor will keep you alive long enough to spend it. If you're the cautious type, it wouldn't hurt to pick up some spares as well. You never know when you might wake up to find that your armor has been stolen, or your sword has been eaten by moths. If you managed to secure a legendary weapon or suit of armor as a boon, gift, or rare treasure, all the better, as you'll have extra money to spend on other things instead (though a spare still wouldn't hurt).

Of course, you shouldn't neglect consumable items either. Potions, ethers, smoke bombs, holy water, whole roasted chickens, and the like can all prove invaluable in a pinch. The more the better; just make sure you have a way to carry them all. If you're lucky, you may find yourself gifted with an innate magical inventory that can store all manner of items with no regard for size and weight. Even better, many models include a handy time distortion feature that not only prevents decay, but keeps your food and drinks just as hot or cold as they were when you stored them. If not, you might be able to find or buy a bag or accessory with a similar effect. Unfortunately, not all fantasy worlds are that convenient, in which case you'll have to either limit yourself to what you can easily carry, or force a party member to lug all of your stuff around for you (contrary to what you might expect, cute little girls tend to be extremely good at carrying large bags of supplies).

Finally, don't hesitate to upgrade any and all of your equipment and supplies the moment something better becomes available. You'll frequently come across more powerful weapons, armor, and even consumables, so try not to become too attached to any of your gear. +10 Attack trumps sentimental value any day. Better to sell your old stuff back to the store to help fund your next shopping spree.

Gotta Craft 'Em All

While shopping for equipment is all well and good, sometimes the more rare and powerful items can only be obtained by crafting, or synthesizing them yourself. Crafting systems are more common in game worlds or those with game elements, but even standard and dark fantasy worlds may contain some form of magical crafting, such as alchemy or fusion. Before going further, it's important to note that, for the purposes of this guide, we're focusing strictly on magical crafting systems. While you could technically spend years training as a blacksmith in order to learn how to forge your own sword and armor, the dark lord probably isn't going to wait around until you're a master smith. Creating a sword via a magical crafting or synthesis system however, is, at most, no more complicated than smacking a metal ingot a few times with a hammer, or piling some random objects on top of each other and clapping your hands.

Since you can obtain the necessary raw materials by killing monsters or foraging, creating items and equipment this way tends to be far cheaper than buying them outright. You never know which items will produce the best results, so be sure to grab everything of interest. Monster tails, horns, claws, beaks, skin, bones, blood, and hearts are all known to be useful crafting components, though cutting them free and carrying them around can be rather messy if you don't have a magical inventory. You should also hang on to any interesting stones or pieces of metal you come across. Even the stems, seeds, and buds from various plants can prove invaluable for crafting.

You can likely find a number of crafting recipes in books, and learn more from people you meet on your journey. However, there's nothing wrong with being creative and using your own intuition. For example, if you did get stuck with a goddess in your party, try cutting off some strands of hair when she's not paying attention, and using them to strengthen your weapons and armor. Gems and rare metals are also excellent choices. Sometimes, it may just be a matter of combining lots of the same item together. Though you should be careful not to waste especially rare crafting materials as, should your recipe fail, they'll likely end up fusing into some sort of worthless goop. But try not to let your failures get you down. Keep at it, and you're bound to end up with that Infinity +2 sword eventually.

Monster Husbandry

If you ended up in a world that focuses on monster training, or your class abilities give you access to a pet or familiar, you may discover that

Collecting materials from fallen monsters is a vital part of an adventurer's job. After all, you wouldn't want to let that dragon spleen go to waste.

increasing the power of your new furry (or scaly, sparkly, or squishy) friends is just as useful, if not more so, than increasing your own. Such creatures, whether physical or magical in nature, can train, grow stronger, and learn new skills the same way you can (specific details will depend on the world). If certain conditions are met, they may even be able to spontaneously evolve into more powerful forms (yes that goes against many laws of science but it's Darwin's fault for neglecting to visit the fantasyverse during his research). You'll likely meet your first monster/pet shortly after arriving in your new world, or perhaps after learning a certain skill in the case of familiars. From then on, it will be your constant companion, whether you want it or not.

In a world with a strong tradition of monster training, you'll likely need to form a team of several monsters, which come in a number of different varieties and elemental affinities (often with a Rock, Paper, Scissors system of strengths and weaknesses). Your long-term goal should be to form a powerful and balanced team with a wide variety of skills that can handle any sort of enemy, or other dangerous situation. However, the best monsters tend to live in remote areas or require rare materials to summon, so building your dream team will take significant time and effort, often being one of the main focuses of your journey. In the short term, however, unless there's a rule in place that prevents it, you should quickly capture as many different monsters as possible. You may not have all of your favorites, but an empty slot in your party isn't helping in the least. Remember, the good team you can have now is far preferable to the perfect team that you may never have. Besides, you can always replace the weaker monsters over time as your collection grows. Or, you can just amass a force of thousands of slimes. Because, why not?

However, if you're limited to a single pet or familiar, your goal should be to have it compliment your own skills and cover any weaknesses. Are you a fireball throwing mage? Get a pet that's good at tanking or melee attacks to keep the giant toads away from you between spells. Perhaps you're a powerful swordsman? How about a pet that can hang back and heal you, or harry your enemies with long range attacks? You like lightning spells? Maybe you can find a pet that drenches its foes in water, making them extra vulnerable to your electricity. Do you just hate walking everywhere? There's probably a pet that you can ride instead. Worried you might run out of food? While certain organizations frown upon it, some pets are actually quite tasty.

Regardless of how many monsters you have, or what their abilities are, it's important to take proper care of them. Most pets and monsters (aside from some purely magical varieties) need food, water, rest, and even medical attention just like animals on Earth. If you don't treat them properly, your monsters may leave, or turn on you at an opportune moment. Even if they're prevented from doing so by some sort of magical coercion, they still won't be able to fight at their full potential if they're not well cared for. So be sure to dedicate a large portion of your budget for proper food, medicine, and the like. And, above all, be

With the right pet, you can ride everywhere in style. Just watch out for salt monsters...

friendly. You want your monsters to like you enough that they'll willingly risk their lives in battle just because you said to. A good trainer shares a bond with his or her monsters that goes both ways. With enough TLC, these creatures could quickly become your best friends for life. Or, at least until you replace them with the stronger monsters you catch later in your journey.

If, on the other hand, you're a summoner, you'll have things much easier. Summoned monsters tend to only hang around long enough to get in a few attacks or spells before returning home (odds are, you pulled them away in the middle of a favorite TV show or a pleasant lunch), so you don't need to worry about raising and caring for them. You will, however, probably need to form contracts with them before they'll answer your calls. This process typically involves either obtaining some sort of rare item, or the old fantasyverse staple of beating them into submission.

Finally, it's worth noting that, while the power and abilities of some trained monsters is tied into your own, in many monster training worlds there's really no need for you to provide anything beyond care and a bit of battle strategy. Inhabitants of such worlds are so used to letting their monsters do all the work for them that even the most evil villain will immediately give up and go home after his team of thematically appropriate monsters is defeated. Just don't assume that this is the case by default. While it is fairly common, there are also a number of worlds where trainers contribute every bit as much to battle as their monster companions, so be ready to fight back, or at very least evade the enemy's attacks, as needed.

Magic and Mechs

While you're far more likely to find yourself piloting a giant robot or mech if you travel far into the future (as covered in *So You've Been Chosen as the Pilot of a Giant Robot*), there are a handful of worlds in the fantasyverse that take a bit more influence from their sci-fi counterparts than is normally allowed. Some of them have been known to summon heroes from Earth, so even if you end up in a fantasy world, being called on to pilot a mech isn't entirely outside the realm of possibility. Of course, these mechs will operate via some sort of magic, rather than computers and electricity (remember, sufficiently complex magic is indistinguishable from technology). But, in practice, that makes surprisingly little difference beyond the fact that you might need a certain level of magical potential in order to be a pilot. So, if you truly want to prepare for everything, it might not hurt to work a bit on your piloting skills (mech simulation games and heavy machinery being the best options) while you're still on Earth.

You can expect fantasy mechs to follow a similar class structure to humans in regard to their skills and abilities, either by design or by adopting and enhancing the existing abilities and spells of their pilots. These mechs can be upgraded via traditional or magical means in order to grow stronger and gain new abilities. They can also respond to their pilot's emotional state, activating special powers or transformations if the pilot becomes particularly angry or distressed. That said, unlike with sci-fi mech pilots, an extreme amount of angst is generally not a desired personality trait, and can potentially cause your mech to transform into

71

an out-of-control dark god. Unfortunately, fantasy mechs universally lack an emergency shut-off switch (the fantasyverse board of safety and oversight has, for some reason, yet to create a set of regulations for giant robots) so said transformation is guaranteed to be far more trouble than it's worth.

In addition to the off-the-shelf variety, there will be various legendary mechs scattered about the world, either sealed away or in the hands of certain powerful individuals. Unlike sci-fi worlds, which often feature extremely powerful prototypes, legendary mechs were created long ago using rare components and lost magic, and often have some sort of connection to either the gods or the elemental forces that make up the world. Chances are, you'll get your hands on at least one these over the course of your journey, either via a convenient bit of deus ex machina early on, or in the late stages of your adventure as an upgrade to your regular mech (which probably just got destroyed anyway).

As a plus, compared to their science-based counterparts, fantasy mechs are easy to care for. They require no fuel (beyond the pilot's magical energy), and can generally be repaired instantly via healing magic, without the need for a proper mechanic. If you have a magical inventory, you'll also be able to store your mech inside, bypassing all the usual complications that arise in regard to transportation and stealth when you're trying to take a 50-foot-tall robot everywhere. After all, even as a legendary hero, people will get tired of you destroying the city after the first half-dozen times.

≡ 9 ≡

Forming Your Party

Please note that this chapter refers to parties as in groups of people united on a common quest, not parties as in celebrations with cake and presents. Those are good too (assuming the cake isn't a lie), but far less useful during your fantasy world adventures.

A good party provides many benefits. They can provide you with local knowledge and guidance, cover your weaknesses in battle, become potential love interests, carry your stuff, save you when you get kidnapped, act as backup singers, and be sacrificed to protect you from powerful enemies. Of course, some party members and compositions can end up being more trouble than they're worth. So, if you want your new fantasy world life to go as smoothly as possible, you'll need to put some serious thought into your party composition.

You (Probably) Can't Do It Alone

While there is a certain level of romanticism in the concept of the lone hero, in reality even the most taciturn and anti-social heroes in the fantasyverse tend to amass a party of some sort sooner or later. Whether they're called party members, friends, subordinates, underlings, or "those annoying guys who keep following me around," there's little to no practical difference in the role they serve. True lone heroes are an extreme rarity, and the few that can be found are virtually all gruff barbarian anti-heroes who still manage to amass a network of trusted friends and contacts that they rely on from time to time.

Of course, gruff and barbarian are not words that are often used to describe people summoned from Earth. At present, there are virtually no known accounts of summoned or reincarnated heroes who successfully completed their journeys and saved the world on their own. Even if you try your best to rebuff all potential party members, whether by physical avoidance or by being an insufferable jerk to everyone around you, you're still pretty much guaranteed to amass a group of loyal party members sooner or later, even if you would actually be better off without them. The most you can do is delay the inevitable.

If you're absolutely determined to go it alone, your best chance of pulling it off would be in a dark fantasy world, due to their penchant for lonely brooding heroes and the extremely high odds of any party members you do pick up getting killed off sooner or later. However, no matter how anti-social you may be, the downsides to living in a dark fantasy world greatly outweigh any benefits you might receive by maintaining your privacy. Besides, without loyal ~~meat-shields~~ party members you can ~~sacrifice~~ rely on to protect you from the world's countless dangers, you probably won't live long enough to enjoy your alone time.

The Who's Who of Party Members

The exact composition of your party will vary based on your gender and the type of fantasy world you're in, but it will generally be composed of one to five individuals (any beyond that number are likely disposable tag-alongs, as opposed to true party members) chosen from the following types. (Do note that not every party will include members of each type, and may even contain multiple members of the same type.)

- Companion(s) from Earth
  - If you were able to bring a friend or relative with you from Earth (see Chapter 2), or you got pulled into a fantasy world as part of a group, any companions that haven't been kidnapped or decided to form parties of their own will inevitably join you instead, and will likely overlap with one of the other character types listed here. Except for your mom. If she came along, she'll be so awesome that she defies definition.
- Wise Old Man
  - Note that "old" doesn't necessarily mean elderly and bearded (though that's quite often the case), it could just as easily refer to some middle-aged guy who won't appreciate being referred to as "old man." Either way, expect him to be a fount of useful(?) knowledge about the world and life itself. He may also be a grizzled veteran of some sort, and will probably be your

9. *Forming Your Party*

Choose from a wide variety of quirky and dubiously useful party members!

guide (see Chapter 4). Do note that he's likely to heroically sacrifice himself to save you sooner or later, so make sure that the other members of your party can step up to fill in the gap afterwards. In case you're wondering, wise old women never become party members, preferring instead to give out mysterious advice while hanging out in dark alleys or remote cottages.

- Troubled Hottie
  - Always the opposite gender of the hero (you, presumably), and very attractive. These forlorn girls or angsty guys are lonely, likely friendless, and have a terrible weight on their shoulders. The female version may overlap with the mysterious girl, while the male may overlap with the total emo or jerk with a heart of gold. Either way, the troubled hottie might be your guide, and is guaranteed to be a potential romantic interest. You may even end up with more than one of them in your party. Keep in

75

mind that whatever mysterious issue is troubling each of your
hotties will come out eventually (likely at the worst possible
time), leaving you to go to great lengths in order to sort it out.
In extreme cases, solving one of their problems may even be
the main goal of your journey. Or it might just be a huge pain
in the ass. Either way, it's unavoidable.

- Mysterious Girl
  - She may be cute, beautiful, troubled, upbeat, emo, airheaded,
    or even seemingly emotionless, but she is, above all,
    MYSTERIOUS. Where is she from? Where are her parents?
    Who or what is she, really? And, most importantly, why are
    powerful villains out to capture her? It will take some time,
    but you're sure to learn all the answers eventually, given that
    protecting her and helping her fulfill her destiny is guaranteed
    to be one of the main focuses of your adventure. Depending on
    your gender and her age (not to mention the rating standards
    of the fantasy world in question), she might also be a potential
    romantic interest. Party members of this type are exclusively
    female. Their counterpart, mysterious boys, have long since
    become extinct in the fantasyverse as they weren't cute or
    beautiful enough to attract any protectors.
- Upbeat Adventurer
  - Party members of this type can be male or female and belong
    to any class. They may also overlap with many of the other
    listed types. Upbeat adventurers' defining characteristic
    is their extreme cheerfulness. No matter how bad the
    situation, they'll be the ones to keep the party going with
    their unshakable positivity and can-do attitude. Either
    that, or they'll drive everyone else crazy with their entirely
    unwarranted optimism. Assuming proper age and gender,
    such party members can also make good romantic interests,
    at least so long as you can put up with an endless stream of
    motivational-poster-worthy quotes.
- Friendly Rival
  - Unlike a more traditional rival, a friendly rival doesn't live to
    defeat you. He or she merely sees you as a worthy challenger
    aiming for ever greater heights. If the going gets tough,
    you can be sure that your rival will be there to lend a hand,
    whether traveling with you the entire time, or just popping in

periodically over the course of your adventure. Males tend to be upbeat "bro" types, while females will likely be a bit bitchier (but still care for you deep down). In the rare case that you get a rival of the opposite gender, he or she will eventually become a potential romantic interest. However, be aware that, sooner or later, your rival is going to be defeated by a powerful new enemy and then guilt you into getting revenge so it might be best not to get too involved.

- Loyal Servant
  - As a summoned or reincarnated hero, saving people's lives is par for the course. You do it because it's the right thing to do, not for the reward. Which is good, because there often isn't any. Maybe you'll get an occasional potion or free night at an inn, but that's about the most you can hope for. However, in rare circumstances, someone will feel so indebted to you that he or she will become your loyal servant, eager to follow and aid you in any way possible. How useful your new servant actually is varies. Some servants may be excellent at everything they do, deftly handling domestic tasks while serving as stalwart allies in battle. Others may be lethal chefs, turning even the most basic recipes into deadly poison, and be unable to tell one end of a sword from the other. In the case of the latter, your servant will probably overlap with the cute thing, so at least you can get some comic relief, and maybe fanservice, out of the deal. If your servant is of the appropriate gender, expect him or her to fall madly in love with you, though you're not obligated to reciprocate.

- Grizzled Veteran
  - Party members of this type have been there, done that, and gotten the t-shirt (or scars) to prove it. As such, they tend to be quite knowledgeable, and also very useful in battle. Having multiple veterans in your party can actually be an advantage. They will, however, tend to be a lot older than you and your other party members (except for any wise old men). Another thing to note is that their past experience will sometimes leave them rather jaded and world-weary, causing them to overlap with the jerk with a heart of gold. Veterans of this type are normally grizzled, middle-aged men, but you might encounter the rare tough as nails warrior woman as well. As a side note, if

someone needs to perform a heroic sacrifice for the sake of the party and you don't have a wise old man handy, the grizzled veteran is a good second choice.

- Haughty Noble
  - Sons and daughters of nobility tend to be extremely confident and self-important, looking down on everyone around them. If you have a haughty noble in your party, get ready to listen to countless rants about how great he or she is, and how lacking you are by comparison. Sometimes your noble's much vaunted skills will live up to the hype, but more often they'll range somewhere between mediocre and entirely non-existent. At best, you can expect a slightly annoying, but still very useful party member. As worst, a whiny useless brat. If a male haughty noble becomes a possible romantic interest, expect lots of bragging and flowery lines while he acts as a rather stuck-up Prince Charming. If female, she'll be a full-on tsundere, berating you one moment only to suddenly turn shy and sweet the next. If you're the type of person who is into that kind of thing, great. If not, you'll probably wish you could push your noble suitor off a cliff.
- Jerk with a Heart of Gold
  - Almost exclusively male, party members of this type may also be troubled hotties or grizzled veterans. While generally a pain in the ass, he's really a good guy deep down, and will come through for you when it counts. Eventually, you'll be able to get him to open up and become a far more pleasant person to be around, but that will take considerable time and effort, so be prepared for the long haul. If the age is right, he'll be a possible romantic interest for female heroes, especially those with a penchant for bad boys.
- Analytical Know-It-All
  - The world's greatest (self-proclaimed) genius, sure to have an opinion on each and every subject, and always ready with a plan. While having a genius around can be quite useful, he or she is likely to be a bit of an insufferable know-it-all as well, which can cause problems with your other party members. Despite their vast knowledge, geniuses also tend to be extremely naive in one or more areas of normal life, especially in regard to the opposite sex, and become flustered quite easily

when such situations arise. While this can be funny to watch, it can also be a very exploitable weakness.

- Questionably Trustworthy Rogue
  - A thief, swindler, or conman with a heart of gold. Or, at least, that's what the rogue would like you to believe. In reality, it's hard to say just where his or her loyalties really lie. Expect a rogue to try and win your trust with a combination of a quick tongue and raw sex appeal. He or she may even be a possible romantic interest, but tread carefully. Some rogues really do have a heart of gold (likely stolen from an underserving owner), and will stick with you through thick and thin. Others will bail, or even betray you outright the moment it's to their advantage to do so. As such, it's recommended that you keep a close watch on your heart, your wallet, and any important artifacts or McGuffins you may be carrying around.
- Total Emo
  - To an emo, the world is dark, depressing, and horrible. There's no friendship or love. Everything is pain. If you're in a dark fantasy world, that's actually a very realistic world view. Elsewhere, emos don't make for the most fun or upbeat party members. With a whole lot of TLC, you might be able to bring an emo out of his or her shell, gaining an "upbeat adventurer," "friendly rival," or "loyal servant" in the process. Alternately, if you're the type that finds dark brooding guys or girls hot, you could skip all that hard work and just treat your emo party member as another potential romantic interest.
- Major Airhead
  - This party member doesn't really know where you're going, what you're doing, or even what day of the week it is but she (or, less commonly, he) is determined to stay by your side to the end. Despite being seriously lacking in areas such as IQ and general awareness, airheads are often surprisingly skilled in some form of combat, overlapping with the upbeat adventurer or powerhouse, making them reliable, if somewhat frustrating, members of your party. An airhead can make for a decent romantic interest as well, though getting her to understand your feelings can be a real challenge, so be prepared to hammer it in (perhaps literally).

- Powerhouse with a HUGE Drawback
  - A beautiful goddess blessed with divine power. A mighty ancient dragon whose breath can incinerate an army. A legendary undefeated gamer. A sorceress capable of wielding the most powerful destructive spell known to man. An ultra-high-level monk with a lifetime of battle experience. Why wouldn't you want people like them on your team? What if I told you that one is a complete idiot, one a masochistic pervert, one has crippling social anxiety, one runs out of steam after a single attack, and one is the wrong gender for your harem? Party members of this type boast one or more incredible powers and, in some cases, could almost save the world without your help. However, there's always a rather major "but" involved. They're most common in comic fantasy worlds, where they could easily make up your entire party, but you can expect mountains of frustration with even a single one on your team. That said, his or her skills just might be worth it.
- (Probably Useless) Cute Thing
  - While a party member of this type might occasionally be human or humanoid (likely a cute little girl), it's more likely to be some type of magical creature, such as a fairy or winged cat. It might be your guide but, if not, its main role is going to be standing (or flying) around and looking really cute while serving as an unofficial mascot for your party. Don't expect it to provide any real help in battle, or anything else for that matter. That said, there is a chance that, towards the end of your journey, the cute thing will reveal its true form as an all-powerful dragon, an avatar of the gods, or an extremely attractive naked woman, just in time to save you and the rest of your party from some sort of great peril. Unfortunately, not everyone is that lucky. Feel free to hope for the best, but don't expect much or you'll probably end up disappointed.

A Balancing Act

While you can form a party with any combination of the previously listed types without problem (though some are certainly easier to deal with than others), you do need to take everyone's classes and skills into account, especially your own. In general, a party is considered well-balanced if it contains a warrior or other close-range melee fighter, a defender, a healer, and a magician (or, in a world where magic is rare, an archer or other ranged attacker). Depending on the world and your quest, you might also want party members who are more specialized. For example, having a paladin or a more offensive-minded white mage is invaluable when fighting an army of the undead, while a thief or ninja is a huge help if you find yourself frequently needing to infiltrate enemy bases. Or, if you end up in a more musically inclined world, you might want to prioritize party members with decent singing voices.

In contrast, a party primarily composed of healers may not die easily, but they're also going to have a very hard time defeating their enemies. Similarly, a party of swordsman could be helpless when faced with archers, mages, or aerial foes. Perhaps you have the chance to recruit a very powerful water mage, but the invading army of fishmen are all but immune to his spells.

If possible, your party should be as balanced as possible so you can support each other's strengths, cover each other's weaknesses, and be ready for any conceivable threat or challenge that may arise along your journey. However, as with your own skills, a bit of creativity can often go a long way, and uncover situations where even seemingly useless party members will have their chance to shine (except for the cute thing). They might not shine very brightly or for very long, but if you're stuck with them, you might as well find some use for their talents, however questionable they may be.

Swipe Left

Unfortunately, you don't always get a say in who joins your party. You might get stuck with an undesirable party member due to politics, or because he or she is somehow vital to your quest. Or, you might just end up with "the thing that won't leave," without any viable way to get rid of it (short of murder, which is generally frowned upon when it involves your own party members). Hopefully though, when a potential new party member pops up, you'll have at least some say in the matter. The following party member types are best avoided if at all possible.

With party members like these, maybe going alone is a better idea after all...

- Giant Wuss
  - Regardless of how strong he or she is, this party member is such a complete and total wimp that you can't expect even the tiniest bit of help in combat. At the first sign of danger, the wuss will either run away screaming, or curl up into a little ball and cry. While he or she might have some other useful skills, unless you ended up in one of the rare fantasy worlds with a non-combat related alternate victory condition (see Chapter 16), you'll be fighting so many battles that having a giant wuss in your party is more trouble than it's worth.

- Barely Contained Bundle of Rage
  - Party members of this type are ready to erupt into a berserk frenzy at the drop of a hat. Actually, you probably won't even need to drop your hat. Just existing in the same general vicinity is probably enough. Some may gain a massive anger-induced power boost (complete with optional green coloring), while others will just flail around in an amusingly worthless fashion. The sheer power of the former can be useful at times, but having a walking powder keg on your team is likely to lead to far more injuries and property damage than you want to deal with.
- Jerk with a Heart of Jerk
  - Some people use their gruff or even nasty personality to hide their true feelings and insecurities. With others, what you see is what you get. Some jerks simply enjoy being assholes and have no desire to change. Spend a little time with one, and it's usually not hard to tell the difference. If you suspect that you're dealing with a true jerk through and through, don't try to ascribe some sort of deep meaning or tragic backstory to his actions, just ditch him the moment the opportunity presents itself. As a note, while most party members of this type are male, there is the occasional female version, though she'll often be referred to by a far less flattering title.
- Self-Righteous Asshole
  - See Paladins (Chapter 6). Truly self-righteous people are certain that everything they do and believe is completely and utterly correct. Anyone who dares disagree is either misguided at best, or purely evil at worst. Logic doesn't matter. Facts don't matter. Changing their minds is near impossible and, if you do succeed, there's a high chance that the shock will cause a dangerous mental breakdown. This entirely inflexible way of thinking is sure to cause serious problems sooner or later on your adventure, possibly leading to a violent split in your party. Better to just avoid bringing such people along to begin with. As a note, it's actually fairly common for summoned heroes to fall victim to this mentality as well. The end result is never pretty (in fact, it's often quite painful), so be sure to watch yourself and keep an open mind.
- Simpering Sycophant
  - A complete and total suck-up who spends every minute

of every day kissing your ass (or perhaps that of another party member). At first, you might actually appreciate his or her extreme adoration, but eventually it's bound to cause trouble with the rest of your party, and lead to a bad case of overconfidence. Many sycophants also make for fair-weather friends, and will abandon you when the going gets tough. Better an honest, reliable party member, even if you don't always agree.

- Flaming Pervert
  - If you end up encountering a potential party member of this type, you can expect skimpy outfits, double entendres galore, and an endless supply of bad pick-up lines ranging from mildly amusing, to truly disturbing. If the particular pervert is attractive enough, you may be tempted to keep him or her around for a while. Just remember that, while all the fanservice and innuendo might be fun at first, it'll probably get very annoying over time, and is guaranteed to give others a rather twisted view of your party. Even worse, you may encounter a flaming pervert who is extremely old, the wrong gender, or even the wrong species, providing a constant source of creepiness and truly disturbing visuals. Your best defense is to run away screaming.
- Regular Dude with a HUGE Drawback
  - A powerhouse with a huge drawback might be worth recruiting as his or her incredible skills can often make up for the equally incredible downside. But, if the person's skills aren't especially impressive, there's really no reason to deal with whatever big problem he or she has.
- Weak Noob
  - It might make sense to recruit some weak, inexperienced party members early on in your journey when it's still safe, so you can work on increasing your power and skills together (though starting out with a high-powered ringer is still preferable). Later on though, adding party members who are considerably weaker than the rest of your team is just asking for trouble. You'll have to expend considerable time and effort keeping them safe, and they'll probably just end up getting kidnapped anyway.
- Obvious Traitor
  - A good spy or traitor is cautious, acting as the most dedicated

and loyal of friends until the right moment comes to turn and stab you in the back. People like that are near impossible to identify ahead of time, and the only thing that can save you is a mixture of luck, genre-savviness, and extreme caution. Then there's these guys. Evil color scheme? Check. Evil facial hair (for guys)? Check. Sexy evil outfit (for girls)? Check. Evil laugh? Check. Frequently caught talking about how he or she loves being evil and can't wait to betray you? Check and double check. The moment you meet someone like this, knock him out, tie him up, and throw him in jail (or the nearest volcano). You'll save yourself a whole lot of trouble.

- Person Your Mom Doesn't Like
  - If you managed to bring your mom with you from Earth, be sure to get her opinion about any potential party members. If she has misgivings about someone, then go ahead and move on. Sure, it might be frustrating, but she only has your best interests at heart and, deep down, you know that she's probably a better judge of character than you are. Not to mention that, if you go against her, she'll probably guilt you about it for the rest of your adventure.

≋ 10 ≋

Surviving and Thriving
in a Standard Fantasy World

Note: Chapters 10–13 are designed to provide advice and guidance specific to the type of fantasy world you find yourself in. However, as there are a number of fantasy worlds that combine elements from two or more world types, it is highly recommended that you read all four chapters to ensure that you are perfectly prepared.

Standard fantasy worlds are the bread and butter of the fantasy-verse, and your genre-savviness will serve you well here. The general advice given in Chapters 3 and 4 should be enough to get you off to a reasonable start, combined with the aid of your guide or mentor. However, there are a number of things you can do to make your journey as smooth as possible.

Survive to Thrive

Your risk of dying soon after arriving in a standard fantasy world is rather low, but just be ready for the possible introductory battle, and respond accordingly depending on the situation and your opponents' strength. However, there are some early steps you can take to further improve your chances.

Starting Off on the Right Foot

First, make sure to note whether or not you've accidentally made a rival, or even archenemy early on. Ideally, you should try and avoid doing so, but that isn't always possible. You can, however, keep your eyes open and identify your foes from the start to avoid being caught off-guard. Have your otherworldly knowledge and skills displaced a

While ending up on the run is unavoidable at times, it's certainly not the way you want to start out your adventure.

powerful warrior or noble? If so, there's at least a 50 percent chance that he'll devote all his time and energy to defeating or discrediting you. Are you the prophesied hero that everyone has been waiting for? You can bet that the villain also knows about said prophecy, and is eager to nip it in the bud (probably by stabbing you in the gut). Perhaps you accidentally crushed a pointy-toed witch when you arrived? Don't be surprised when her family, friends, and flying monkeys are all out for your head. And that's only the start. Just assume that anything you did during the start of your adventure that, intentionally or unintentionally, harmed or humiliated someone else, will probably come back to bite you (perhaps literally).

The Summon Clause

If you were summoned to the world by a king, mage, demon lord, or really anything other than a god or goddess, your next step should be to determine the situation surrounding your summoning.* Of course, you'll need to know what your summoner expects of you (likely some variation of either saving the world, or being his or her loyal servant). But you also need to read all the metaphorical fine print.

Furthermore, some summoning spells include a magical contract that binds the summoned party (you) to the will of the summoner. While sometimes simply a means of ensuring the summoner's own safety, more unprincipled individuals and nations have been known to summon large numbers of people from Earth to use to as powerful slaves for both labor and combat. If you find yourself in such a situation, don't immediately rebel. You're not Spartacus (besides— *SPOILER ALERT*—he died). It's better to keep your head down, be polite, and follow orders. As you're doing so, keep your eyes and ears open. Such contracts always feature either a loophole (examine the wording very carefully), or some way they can be annulled. Powerful mages can be of use in that regard, or you might even be able to remove or resist the control spell on your own once you've grown strong enough. Unfortunately, people who are unscrupulous enough to use summoning spells in this way generally don't treat their otherworldly servants especially well, so make finding a means of escape your top priority. You can worry about figuring out your main quest (which will quite likely involve defeating whoever summoned you) later on.

Even if no magical control or coercion is involved, your summoner still might try to take advantage of you in other ways, especially in power struggles between competing kingdoms or factions. Listen closely when you're told about the situation and why you were

---

* Fantasyverse Surgeon General's Warning: Otherworldly summoning has been known to cause various negative side effects such as vomiting, nausea, and potentially fatal imbalances of magical energy. To avoid exploding, please report any such symptoms to your local cleric.

summoned. If possible, seek confirmation from some normal towns-people or other unaffiliated parties. Observe everything and everyone carefully, and try to read between the lines. If something seems fishy, it probably is (doubly true if the information comes from an actual fish). You can, of course, try to get to the bottom of it on your own, but that can be dangerous. At times it's better to simply cut and run. Besides, you'll no doubt end up having to deal with whatever corrupt mages or nobility summoned you eventually, so all the better to do it after you've had a chance to power up a bit.

If, on the other hand, you traveled to a fantasy world via a portal or reincarnation (which is handled exclusively by the gods), you shouldn't have to worry about any of the aforementioned situations. However, people may still try to take advantage of you, especially if your powers and/or knowledge are especially valuable in your new world, so it never hurts to be cautious when meeting strangers, especially if they're seek-ing your help.

Bulking Up

Once you're safe, set aside a bit of time for training. In worlds with video game elements, you can likely spend a while level-grinding by kill-ings large numbers of weaker monsters. Staying ahead of the level curve will help keep you from getting overwhelmed during the course of your adventures. In more traditional fantasy worlds, however, you'll have to increase your skills through good old-fashioned training. Make a point of finding one or more instructors specializing in the type of weapons, magic, or other skills that you plan to use, and devote yourself to learn-ing as much as possible. Royal courts (if you've been summoned or oth-erwise acknowledged by the royal family) and guilds are a good place to find suitable instructors. While you won't become a master archer or magician overnight, a few weeks or even a few days of good training can make a huge difference.

And don't just focus on weapons. When it comes down to it, if you get ripped, there are few problems that can't be solved by sheer force. Of course, building muscle mass takes considerable time and energy. And, unlike certain professional sports leagues, the fantasyverse is rather lacking in steroids. However, you might be able to use magic to speed up the process by deliberately working yourself to the point of collapse, and then magically regenerating your muscles at a rapid pace. Repeat this a few times, along with some properly balanced meals, and you can easily cram a week's worth of bodybuilding into a single day.

The Bare Necessities

Of course, you'll also need to secure food and lodging. (And clothes, assuming you're not taking the "bare" part of bare necessities a bit too literally.) If you've got an "in" with the royal family, or another influential person or group, they'll likely provide everything you need. If not, you'll have to pay for it yourself. If you were able to bring some gold with you from Earth, that should cover things for a while, but sooner or later you'll need to start earning an income of your own. Monster hunting is a common way to do so. Though, unlike in game worlds, monsters probably won't be carrying large sacks of money around with them. Some, however, may have bounties on their heads. You should also be able to sell those heads, and various other body parts, to the local guilds or crafters. Certain plants, stones, and other items can similarly be hunted and sold. Expect the adventurer's guild (if present) to have information and even formal quests available. You may also be able to leverage any special skills you've gained to your advantage by magically synthesizing rare items, cooking delicious Earth food, or transporting large burdens via your magical inventory. More traditional jobs are an option as well. Finally, if your quest doesn't allow you to stay in one place for any length of time, you can always put your survival skills to use, sleeping under the stars (and the rain clouds) while hunting and cooking your own meals. Though, in such cases, you'll want to at least secure some decent camping gear first.

Thrive to Survive

After you've gotten settled and made some progress on your quest, you might think that everything else should be fairly simple. After all, compared to starting over again in a new world, defeating some big bad monster or evil empire (see Chapter 16 for more detailed information) should be simple enough, right? Even rebuilding a kingdom or founding your own couldn't be too hard (at least not so long as you've read Chapter 15). However, there are still some things you should do and watch out for in order to ensure that a new enemy or sudden plot twist doesn't throw a wrench (or a bottle of deadly poison) into your plans.

Don't Forget Leg Day (or Arm Day, or Sword Day, or Spell Day, or...)

First, and most importantly, don't neglect your training. The more successful you become, and the further you travel away from your starting location, the stronger the enemies that you'll face. Fortunately, fantasyverse labor laws dictate that the strength of monsters and other enemies that any hero faces is required to start out low and gradually increase over time. Therefore, you and your party should be able to defeat anything that comes at you, though sometimes only via an exciting skin-of-your-teeth victory. If you ever encounter an enemy that is clearly far, far beyond your current skills, then you simply need to survive and either hold it back, or run away until you're saved in a suitably dramatic way by a powerful warrior, a heroic sacrifice, or a bit of deus ex machina.

However, that only applies if you've been steadily training and increasing your own strength and ability. The power of your enemies scales relative to time, distance, and progress on your main quest. It does not, strictly speaking, scale in accordance with your actual power level. As such, if you manage to fit in enough extra training, you may discover that even the stronger foes that you face aren't too much of a threat. On the other hand, if you slack off, you're likely to find yourself struggling against even weaker enemies.

Dirty Rotten Traitors

You should always watch out for traitors or other forms of betrayal. In comic fantasy worlds, any potential spy or traitor is always of the extremely obvious type (see the list of party members to avoid in Chapter 9). And in dark fantasy worlds, you can safely assume that anyone and everyone is apt to betray you given the right opportunity. In standard fantasy worlds, however, it's actually rather easy to get caught off-guard by a smart, cautious traitor. Genre-savviness and a keen sense of observation are your best friends here. Even true masters of deception are apt to slip up from time to time, if only slightly. You can't expect to catch them cackling evilly about their plans or wearing an "I Love

Evil" t-shirt, but an errant glance or minor slip of the tongue can still give them away if you're sharp enough. It's also important to remember that not all traitors are working for the evil empire, demon lord, or the like. Many are, sure, but even during times of great crisis, there are people who will gladly risk dooming the entire world so long as it advances their own pursuit of money and power. So just because the vizier isn't a literal monster in disguise (though that's quite common as well), that doesn't mean he isn't waiting for a chance to stab you in the back.

Unfortunately, no matter how observant you are, some traitors are too skilled and careful to ever slip up or leave any hints as to their true intentions, no matter how closely you look. However, there are still ways to reduce or even fully mitigate the damage that they can cause. The first is via genre-savviness. In the fantasyverse, some individuals are simply more likely than others to betray you. The aforementioned obvious traitor aside, the next most likely person to betray you is the second-in-command. It doesn't really matter whether he's second in command of the kingdom, the adventurer's guild, or your favorite restaurant. You could be looking at a vizier, count, assistant manager, or even an actual princess. It's best to automatically be suspicious of anyone you meet who holds such a position, regardless of the circumstances. Or, if you want to be especially pro-active, just automatically accuse every second-in-command of being a traitor the moment you're introduced. You'll be right often enough that people will be willing to forgive the occasional false positive.

The other person that you really need to watch out for is the one who you would absolutely never ever suspect of betraying you. Just look at all your party members, friends, and acquaintances, and decide whom among them couldn't possibly turn on you no matter what. Then watch that person like a hawk. No matter how kind, sweet, and honest he may be, there's still a very real risk that he's an amazing actor, or at least being blackmailed to turn on you. This is especially true if you have an obvious traitor in your midst. A real master of deception will use the obvious traitor (or someone so unlikable that you merely want him to be the obvious traitor) to distract you and the rest of your party so you'll never see the real deception until it's too late. On that note, a supposedly obvious traitor who hasn't shown clear evidence of treason, but is merely suspicious and highly unlikable, is probably entirely trustworthy.

If you're not able to catch a traitor in time, you can also protect yourself by preparing for possible betrayals. Always check for poison in your food and drink (preferably by feeding them to the nearest second-in-command), arrange code words with your closest allies so none of you can be fooled by false messages or imposters, set traps to catch anyone who tries to steal your equipment, and always travel with a companion who can vouch for your activities and whereabouts to counter false accusations of theft or assault. And, of course, remain alert and skilled enough to defend against the traditional knife in the back or arrow in the chest (good armor and healing magic never hurt either). When in doubt, be cautious. Be overly cautious even. Though do keep in mind that, when taken too far, extreme caution can seriously annoy your party members, and even harm your overall reputation, so you'll need to find a balance between safety and sanity.

You've Got a Friend in the Fantasyverse

On Earth, an important part of success is networking. It's not what you know, but who you know, and all that. The same applies in fantasy worlds. Over the course of your adventures, you're sure to encounter kings, nobles, merchants, mercenaries, legendary beasts, and even divine beings. While you'll almost certainly have to kill some of them, the ones that you rescue, or otherwise aid or associate with, will become valuable friends and allies. A merchant can provide you with rare and discounted items and equipment. A king can send his soldiers to your aid. Even a lowly beggar can be an invaluable source of information. As such, try to avoid taking the cold, uncaring, anti-hero approach. Be polite, be friendly, and accept gratitude when it's offered. And, once you've formed a relationship, do your best to maintain it. While that may be difficult if you find yourself traveling frequently, you should still be able to send word from time to time. There's no social media in the fantasyverse, but people on Earth somehow managed to stay in touch before *Facebook* and *Twitter*, so you should be able to figure something out, and sooner or later your efforts will pay off, likely at a critical moment.

Stealing Credit

Finally, take advantage of your knowledge from Earth. While fantasy worlds feature many amazing technical and magical innovations, they're bound to be missing a number of convenient things from your home planet. Capitalizing on your knowledge will not only help you, but

A completely 100 percent original recipe. Any similarity to an extremely popular food back on Earth is entirely coincidental.

the world as a whole. Perhaps you aren't skilled enough to create a fully working electrical power grid or telephone (then again, if you are, go for it), but even something as simple as introducing pizza or mayonnaise could earn you international acclaim, not to mention a small fortune. Bringing something more significant, such as modern agricultural techniques or military theory, could quickly raise you to one of the highest ranks in any government. Though you do need to think carefully before making any such moves. The money and renown any such otherworldly development would bring is bound to be very useful, but will also make it easier for your enemies to keep tabs on your movements. While other advances could be used, whether by your enemies or even your allies, to make the world a much more dangerous place. So, while you do want to take full advantage of your Earthly knowledge, make sure to think carefully about whether or not your new world really needs dynamite or idol singers before you go all in.

⇛ 11 ⇚

Not Being Made a Fool of in a Comic Fantasy World

Comic fantasy worlds are among the safest in the fantasyverse. They also revolve very heavily around tropes and clichés, allowing a genre-savvy hero to predict most major events and dangers long before they happen. They do, however, include a number of unique challenges all of their own, so you need to prepare if you want to avoid being made the constant butt of the world's jokes. As a note, because comic fantasy worlds tend to draw a considerable amount of their inspiration from either traditional fantasy or video game fantasy worlds, it's recommended that you review Chapters 10 and 12 as well.

Avoiding Pratfalls

Unless you have a very specific type of personality, life in a comic fantasy world will likely involve a very steep learning curve, not just due to the fantasy elements, but the comedy as well. Earth essentially operates on a clear set of rules. Whether or not you understand them, there are immutable laws of nature that govern how the world works. The laws of gravity. The laws of physics. The law of everyone hating Brussels sprouts. And so on. Beyond that, even with how unpredictable some people can be, a bit of logic, reason, and common sense can be used to smoothly predict and navigate most social situations. (If you believe that not to be the case, please buy our two-volume combo set containing *So You've Determined That You're the Only Sane Person in the World* and *So You've Come to the Realization That You're a Self-Righteous Asshole*, one of them should help). Comic fantasy worlds, however, tend to tie logic in a knot, throw it out the window, and then dance the mambo while blatantly ignoring the laws of nature, all in the name of a good gag. While other chapters can help you adjust to the fantasy elements of your new home, here are some tips to help you with the more comedic side.

Pardon the Clichés

Clichés are funny. Sometimes in a tired, eye-rolling way, but they do get laughs. As such, comic fantasy worlds are packed full to the brim with cliché places, characters, and situations. If you've seen it before in countless fantasy stories, and it's at least mildly funny, it will almost certainly happen to you sooner or later. For example, when recruiting a party, you can safely assume that every single potential member will come with some sort of extremely quirky personality. You're also certain to encounter lots of places, items, and even people whose names look like they came straight out of *The Big Book of Really Bad Puns*. And when you uncover a villain's evil plan (not necessarily the big bad demon lord or evil emperor, but certainly some of his underlings), expect it to be so incredibly stupid that no one in their right mind would ever think it could work ... and then it does anyway. If you come across an obvious trap, someone will still manage to set it off. If there's a source of mud or slime around, you will get covered in it. If you're a guy and something has the potential to hit you in the balls, it probably will (fortunately, the same can be said for any male enemies). If you're a girl, it's only a matter of time before one of your party members (probably the guy you have a crush on) accidentally trips and smashes his face into your chest, pulls down your skirt, or otherwise knocks the two of you into some sort of embarrassing position. Fortunately, while clichés can be very annoying, they're also extremely predictable so, with a bit of physical and mental preparation, you can often mitigate or even completely avoid the more problematic ones. Once again, your genre-savviness will serve you well.

Expect the Unexpected

While clichés are funny, subverting them can be even funnier. So while it's important to plan for the clichés, a truly prepared hero will also anticipate ways that they could be twisted for even larger laughs. Perhaps the legendary sealed beast will be a cute kitten (which will then proceed to cutely scratch you to death). Maybe you'll successfully evade a big bad trap, only to slip and fall down the stairs right past it. Hoping for a big reward for defeating a venom spewing giant spider? You might, instead, be arrested for killing someone's beloved pet. Did you narrowly avoid a strike to the balls (for guys), or a face to your chest (for girls)? Be ready for an even more painful or embarrassing follow-up. Expect cabbages to fly, frogs to sing, and the power of pizza (or maybe friendship) to save the world. A good comic fantasy world won't pull stunts like this all the time. Instead, it will mix the occasional subversion in among all the standard gags and clichés in order to throw you off your guard. After all, if you're expecting the unexpected, then it really isn't unexpected, now is it? As such, you're best off keeping the possibility that subversions can happen in the back of your mind, so that you're ready to quickly respond to them when they do. If you get too focused on them, then the standard clichés will start catching you off-guard instead, which really isn't any better.

Roll with the Punches

While you might assume that the phrase "roll with the punches" indicates that you should just accept that you're in a comedic world and go along with the craziness (an option that will be covered in the next section), it should actually be taken far more literally. Physical humor is a cornerstone of any comic fantasy world. As such, a punch to the face, kick to the balls, and frying pan to the head are all common occupational hazards for an otherworldly hero. You can also expect to fall down stairs, crash into walls, and have doors opened into your face on a regular basis.

Female heroes actually have a notable advantage in this regard. In addition to not having to worry about the aforementioned kick to the balls, chivalry is still alive and well in much of the fantasyverse. As a result, women tend to fall victim to far fewer physical pratfalls than their male counterparts, and the ones that do pop-up are relatively mild. Females, however, are far more likely to fall victim to fanservice type gags, and end up accidentally flashing or getting groped by their male party members. Please note that such incidents are entirely unintentional, and violently pummeling the perceived offender will only encourage the forces of comedy. Better to either brush the whole thing aside calmly and politely, while keeping your outward signs of embarrassment minimal, or, even better, avoid such situations in the first place by dressing in sensible, hard to remove clothes (including pants and a metal breastplate), and always locking the door before you shower or bathe.

A sensible and hard to remove outfit will automatically defend against 85 percent of embarrassing fanservice gags.

For male heroes, don't expect your female party members to take that advice. They will trip and crash into you (and vice versa) in embarrassing ways while wearing outfits that are one stitch away from a colossal costume failure. You will also accidentally walk in on each other bathing, changing, or otherwise in various states of undress. While that might actually sound rather enjoyable, it's rarely, if ever, worth the consequences. In any such situation, even if it was clearly her fault or a simple accident (which tends to be the case 99.9 percent of the time), you can expect a disproportionately violent response. If you're lucky, you might get off with a mere punch to the face or a kick to the balls. In more extreme cases, the "victim" may deliver such a powerful blow that she sends you flying through walls and soaring off into the sky, followed by an equally painful landing. If she's a mage, you can expect to be frozen, burned to a crisp, or blown up by her spell of choice. Her power, in these situations, will far surpass anything she ever shows in battle. Fortunately, you won't normally suffer any lasting damage from these attacks, no matter how much they hurt at the time. If you're in a world with powerful, easy-to-use healing and/or revival magic, it is actually quite possible that you'll end up seriously injured or even dead from her assault, but you're sure to be patched up quickly. Unfortunately, short of shunning any and all contact with the opposite sex, there is no known method of avoiding or mitigating these situations.

Male or female, you'll be best served by knowing that physical comedy happens, and there's nothing that can be done to avoid the occasional painful punch, kick, or pratfall. Just keep your health up, wear good defensive gear, and try not to overreact. Remember, the whole point of physical gags is to elicit laughs. If your reaction doesn't fit the bill, the world will soon move on to other, more effective forms of comedy.

To Be, or Not to Be the Straight Man

If you find yourself in a comic fantasy world, it's quite natural to fall into the role of the straight man (or woman, if you prefer). The rest of your party, or even the world as a whole, may not bat an eye at all of the ridiculous goings-on but, with your Earthly experiences and perspectives, you simply can't help noticing how utterly stupid and illogical it all is. You may feel like you're the only one who is really taking things as seriously as they deserve. And, to be honest, you may be right. This is a common and valid response to comic fantasy worlds. Playing the straight man will allow you to maintain some level of sanity and dignity no matter how crazy everything gets.* It will also help you keep the rest of your party members on track when the comic goings-on threaten to derail your main quest.

If you have the right personality type, you may be able to take a different approach, and just go along with everything. Give yourself a weird personality quirk. Set yourself up for gags, no matter how painful and/or embarrassing they may be. And, when you end up being the butt of a joke, react (or rather overreact) accordingly. In other words, act like the locals.

---

* Fantasyverse Surgeon General's Warning: Side effects of being a straight man include a growing sense of annoyance and frustration with everyone and everything around you, and an overwhelming desire to bang your head repeatedly against a wall.

Unfortunately, there are no records of any heroes from Earth who have successfully adopted this technique. This could indicate that, no matter how hard they may try, people with at least a base level of logic and common sense simply can't bring themselves to fully accept the rules of a comic fantasy world. It's possible that even the world itself rejects their attempts, ramping up the absurdity until they have no choice but to rail against it. Still, if you find yourself chaffing in the straight man role, it may be worth a try.

Living and Laughing

While life in a comic fantasy world will take some getting used to, once you've fully acclimated there are a lot of things to appreciate, including the relative safety compared to other types of fantasy worlds, and the frequent outbreaks of extreme fanservice for both guys and girls (though you do need to watch out for unexpected bouts of extreme fan disservice as well). Comic fantasy worlds also tend to be among the simplest in which to build a harem, if that's one of your goals (see Chapter 14). Sometimes, the insanity is worth it. However, there are still things you should be aware of even after the initial adjustment period is over.

Make the Comedy Work for You

Once you've become familiar with the favored gags and comedic styles of your particular world, you can use them to your advantage. Manipulate the situation so that your enemy will get hit in the face by a door, or fall down the stairs. Even better, set him up for a fanservice gag with the most violent of your female party members, and watch as she pummels the most powerful foes into submission. If people have a tendency to slip on banana peels, carry a few with you at all times to use against any attackers. You can even use them to set a perimeter around your home or camp. If subversion gags are more in-style, get a cute, fluffy little pet that likes to bite the heads off your enemies. If you're especially daring, you could even set yourself up for a particularly violent bit of physical comedy, and then dodge out of the way at the last moment, leaving your foe to become collateral damage. Looking to strike it rich? Bet on the utterly impossible long shot, then encourage your rival to make an opposing bet along with some sort of ridiculously hilarious promise in the minuscule chance that he loses. The more embarrassing it is, the better your odds. As long as you know your comedy, a little bit of creativity can lead to consistently hilarious, and highly beneficial, results.

Sudden Bouts of Drama

Every once in a while, a comic fantasy world finds itself thinking that it isn't being taken seriously enough, resulting in sudden bouts of extreme drama. When this happens, all bets are off. The usual jokes and gags fade into the background, the villains get serious, and someone (specifically one of your friends or allies) is probably going to die. Fortunately, many heroes complete their adventures without ever having to deal with such a drastic tonal shift. Unfortunately, there's no guarantee that you'll be one of them.

You can attempt to stave off this situation by ensuring that, despite all the wacky hijinks you find yourself in, you and your party still manage to have your fair share of epic, challenging battles and heartfelt emotional moments. As long as there is still some drama to be found, the world usually won't feel the need to go off the deep end and bombard you with extreme DRAMA. Failing at that, you can at least do your best to be prepared for the dramatic happenings when they occur. The shift to the dramatic is most likely to take place at roughly the mid-point of your quest, or right near the end, so be extra careful at those points. If it feels like you've gone an unusual length of time without a big gag, or if the world suddenly starts to look a lot scarier and gloomier than it usually does, you can take that as a sign that major drama is about to go down.

Another warning bell is the appearance of a new enemy who sports a much darker and edgier look than anyone you've faced thus far. Be on close guard if such a foe appears, because he'll probably look to prove how serious he is by killing one of your party members. In fact, you may want to try and keep a wise old man around for that very situation. Better him than your budding love interest. If there's no one you want to sacrifice, you could try to turn and run immediately upon the new enemy's appearance. If you pull it off correctly, the forces of comedy may decide that the interruption of his epic introduction is funny enough to let it slide. In fact, comedy can be your best weapon against sudden drama. Set your new, dark enemy up for a dumb gag. Slip and fall face

The sudden appearance of a new "darker and edgier" enemy is surefire sign that s*** is about to hit the fan. Make a run for it while you still can.

first into a party member's cleavage. Pull out a giant loaf of bread instead of your sword. "Accidentally" flash your opponent and then accuse him of being a pervert. If you can successfully suck all the drama and tension out of the situation before anyone dies, the normal comedic rules of the universe should reassert themselves.

Of course, they are called *sudden* bouts of drama for a reason, and sometimes the drama will strike before you have any chance to negate or counter it. That's why it's important to never neglect your training. While comic fantasy worlds are usually less focused on power levels and skills than other types, being a bit overpowered can be the difference between life and death in the case of a rapid tonal shift.

⇛ 12 ⇚

Pwning a Video Game Fantasy World

Though relative newcomers to the fantasyverse, video game worlds have exploded in popularity, quickly becoming go-to destinations for a large number of summoned and reincarnated heroes. Even more traditional fantasy worlds have taken notice, adopting many video game conventions and systems for their own use. As such, even if you're not much of a gamer, you should know your ATK from your DEF, and have a firm understanding of how to grind for EXP before setting out on your adventure.

Don't Be a Noob

For those of you who haven't acclimated yourselves with common gaming lingo, "noob" refers to a new, inexperienced player. While everyone has to start at the bottom, it's a rank that's best left behind as soon as possible, especially when you're actually living the game, rather than sitting comfortably at home with a mouse or controller in hand. It's one thing if your inexperience results in a couple of hours of lost progress, or the ire of your multiplayer teammates. It's another entirely when it can lead to death, destruction, and the end of the world. Fortunately, So You've Guides is here to help. Simply follow our advice, and soon you'll be the one "pwning noobs" rather than the other way around.

Don't Skip the Tutorial

While learning the ropes is important in any type of fantasy world, video game worlds often start you out on your adventures with a proper tutorial. It may take the form of guild-sponsored lessons, or your guide may give you a lengthy lecture on such fascinating topics as menu navigation and sorting the contents of your magical inventory. If you're already an experienced gamer, you may be tempted to skip over such a dull introductory scene. While you may not be able push a button to literally skip the scene or fast-forward through all of the dialogue, walking out works nearly as well. Or, if you'd rather be polite, you can simply thank the teacher but insist that you already know what you're doing. That, however, would be a mistake. Even if you've spent hundreds of hours playing the game on which your new world is based, there's likely at least a few small changes compared to what you're familiar with. No matter how dull the tutorial may be, it's far better to listen all the way through than to end up kicking yourself weeks later because you never learned about that amazing weapon copy feature all of your rivals are using. And even in the worst case, where you don't learn anything of use, a little review never hurts, especially when it's your life on the line.

Know Your Game Systems

Ideally, if you're aiming for a new life in a fantasy world, you should study games and game mechanics while still on Earth, especially RPGs, Action RPGs, and MMORPGs, as they tend to form the basis for most video game fantasy worlds. If your goal is to end up in a particular game world, then you should become as much of an expert on said world as possible, both by playing the game, and by obsessively combing through every strategy site and video available. But perhaps you slacked off or were caught off-guard. While it can be a bit more difficult to learn all the minutia of a game system without internet access, you should still be able to pick up the key points after your arrival. Once you've cleared the aforementioned tutorial, start talking to everyone. And we do mean EVERYONE. You never know which random passerby might share some valuable information about how to maximize your stats, manage your STM, or increase your GLD. Some may even offer additional tutorials. However, be warned that this approach is geared only to true video game worlds. In worlds that are merely based on video games, or borrowing some game elements, all the people you see walking around will be real, living, breathing individuals, rather than digital NPCs. As such, they may look at you rather strangely if you're literally talking to everyone and, in the worst case, might send the local guards after you.

Another approach is to look through your menus (if present). Be sure to read all descriptive text, scrutinize every option, and appraise, scan, or assess every item and ability you possess. You can also use any appraisal skills you may have on the people and things you see. This is useful both for general information gathering, and for learning more about any enemies and allies you encounter. Of course, other people may do the same to you, so picking up a skill that blocks appraisals, or otherwise hides or falsifies your stats, can be quite useful. You should also remember that, unlike in real games, time doesn't freeze when you're looking at your menu, so only do so when it's safe. Nothing's more embarrassing than having your new fantasy world life brought to an early end because you got run over by a carriage or stabbed by a goblin while checking your menu options.

If you're still having trouble learning what you need to know, guilds (especially adventurer's guilds), your guide, and any friends or party members you pick up early on should be able to fill in the blanks if asked. "If asked" being the key word, as much of this information is likely considered common knowledge in your new world so, without some prompting, they'll probably assume that you already know.

Power Leveling for Fun and Profit

While powering up and training are vital in every type of fantasy world, they're especially important in video game worlds where everything revolves around levels and stats. In a world with more realistic combat, even the weakest amateur could defeat a master swordsman or wizard with a lucky blow. But when video game systems come into play, it can be near impossible to even scratch a monster if its stats and/ or level are considerably higher than your own. Gaining levels can also provide additional bonuses such as granting access to new spells and abilities, and even the option to change classes or evolve into a more powerful form (for monsters and inanimate objects).

In almost all cases, the fastest way to gain levels is through combat. Whether or not there's a proper reason behind it, killing monsters (and other humans, for that matter) will cause you to earn EXP (or some other abbreviation) which will increase your level, boosting your stats and abilities in turn. Fortunately, video game worlds have no shortage of monsters. In fact, outside of a town or city, you often can't walk ten steps without a group of them jumping you. If you're environmentally inclined, you might worry that killing large numbers of wild creatures will cause irreparable damage to the local ecosystem. However, quasi-fantastic mathematicians have proven that normal monsters exist as a subset of infinity and, as such, their numbers in a given area will never decrease for any significant length of time. In fact, by culling their numbers, even temporarily, you're helping prevent this infinite hoard from devastating the local non-monstrous flora and fauna. So, there's absolutely no need to feel bad about slaughtering every single monster you lay your eyes on. Besides, they'd gladly do the same to you if given the chance.

Since you're guaranteed to start your adventure in an area with relatively weak monsters, you should take some time to farm (kill) as many as possible in order to get off to a strong start. As an added bonus, most monsters will drop varying amounts of the local currency and/or body parts that can be sold for said currency. While this infinite source of cash doubtless causes untold problems for the world's economy, that's not normally something you'll need to worry about. Eventually, you'll reach the point where killing the local monsters earns you so little EXP that leveling up further could take days or weeks. At that point, feel free to continue with your adventure until you get to the next town or outpost, where you can repeat the process with a stronger set of monsters. However, for the truly patient and cautious, you might be able to take advantage of an effect present in certain true video game worlds known as Protagonist Time Dilation, or PTD. This strange phenomenon causes the world to exist between the cracks in time so that while hours, days, and seasons appear to pass, no one will age, and nothing of any importance will take place until the hero (probably you) has reached certain preset locations. If you've determined that your world suffers from PTD, you can use it to your advantage by farming only the weakest and least dangerous monsters, such as slimes, until you've advanced your level, stats, and abilities to the point where little else in the world can pose any sort of threat. It might take three hundred years, but if you have the patience and mental fortitude, it's certainly the safest way to prepare for your adventure.

Looking for Group

Recruiting party members is something that isn't limited to any particular type of fantasy world but, as video game worlds tend to have much stricter class designations than other parts of the fantasyverse, you need to be extra careful to ensure a balanced party formation. You can see Chapters 6 and 9 for general information about classes and party formation. But if you're in a true video game world, there is an additional factor that must be taken into consideration: whether you plan to recruit other players or NPCs.

NPCs are often easy to recruit, requiring little more than a quick conversation and, perhaps, a share of the loot from your battles. They also come in a wide variety of shapes, sizes, and classes, so you can easily form your party however you like. Just go to the nearest adventurer's guild or tavern, and you're sure to find a few who strike your fancy. The downside of recruiting NPCs is that, as digital, AI-driven lifeforms, their personalities, combat strategies, and general intellect tend to range from moderately competent to abysmal. They also rarely make the best friends or conversation partners. Even when gifted with sci-fi level AI, NPCs will still come across as lacking in some way compared to a true human companion.

Fortunately, true video game worlds often summon multiple heroes at a time, especially in the case of online multiplayer games, so there's a good chance that there will be other real humans around that you can potentially team up with (just make sure to properly identify your role, as discussed in Chapter 5). While it's true that some real people just plain suck, most can be counted on to be far more clever, creative, and engaging than NPCs, and far more likely to learn and grow over the course of your adventure. And, if you all eventually make it back to Earth, you'll be able to continue your friendships (or perhaps deadly rivalries) right where you left off.

Being l33t

It's not enough to merely graduate from being a noob. To truly master your new world, you must rise to the ranks of the few, the proud, the l33t (or, if you prefer, "epic," "pog," or "really groovy"). Sure, you could be one of the countless middle-of-the-road gamers muddling your way through your new life, but why would you settle for that when you could be so much more? Instead, use the following advice to begin your path to l33tness.

So You've Landed in a Fantasy World

Beware the Patches

If you're in a true video game world, that means that, somewhere out there, are one or more developers with the power to update, modify, and patch the world. While they're unlikely to be anything special back on Earth, to inhabitants of the game world, they're essentially on the same level as gods. It's quite likely that, throughout the course of your adventure, they may take it upon themselves to patch the world in various ways. Sometimes, those patches might add additional features and remove bugs. Other times, they may shut down useful exploits (see the next section), nerf your best abilities, or otherwise make your life more difficult. This is especially true if the developers hate you, or are just generally sadistic. Unless you yourself have administrative access and/or extreme hacking powers, there is nothing you can do to actually block or counteract a patch, so you'll just have to do your best to roll with it.

If you're lucky, the developers will make an announcement whenever the game is patched, complete with a list of all the changes that were made. If so, make sure you carefully read it as soon as possible. If no such announcements are made, there will usually still be some sign that the game has been updated (typically some sort of elaborate large-scale visual effect). Watch for these signs and, whenever one occurs, proceed cautiously and check all your items, skills, and the like for any changes. If a patch is applied while you're in the midst of a battle, especially against a boss or similar enemy, you can almost certainly assume that either the boss has received some sort of power up, or whatever methods you've been using to win have been drastically nerfed. If possible, you should retreat for the time being, and reassess the situation before resuming the battle.

As a side note, it's generally best not to think about confronting the developers should they appear in-game. Their avatars are guaranteed to feature max stats and numerous cheat-level abilities, along with some form of invincibility. Only the most arrogant and careless of developers will leave themselves any sort of vulnerability in-game (such as, say, a knife to the back). So, while you can certainly hope that your developers fall into that category, it's far better to wait to confront them until after you've returned to the real world, where they're unlikely to have much of any physical prowess, and will probably break down in tears at the mere threat of violence.

12. *Pwning a Video Game Fantasy World*

Evil game developers and other "keyboard warriors" tend to be far weaker (and considerably wimpier) in the real world.

Finding the Exploits

More so than anywhere else in the fantasyverse, video game worlds are likely to have all sorts of cheats, exploits, and broken strategies you can use to make your adventure easier. While most are discovered entirely by accident, a keen eye, some genre-savviness, and a general knowledge of games and programming can help. For example, try to carry around 100 or 256 of the same item. Use logic bombs such as "this statement is false" on various enemies and NPCs. If you find a controller or keyboard of some sort, punch in Up, Up, Down, Down, Left, Right, Left, Right, B, A, Select, Start.

Do note that not all exploits will produce beneficial results, so it might be best to avoid some of the more extreme options (like logic bombs) outside of emergency situations. Things like maxing out a single stat (such as DEF or SPD), combining abilities that were clearly never meant to be combined, and performing elaborate acrobatic routines to access normally unreachable areas, are fairly safe and could result in shortcuts or OP builds.

Search EVERYWHERE

Whether it's in relation to a side-quest or your main adventure, any decent game world will make it abundantly clear where you need to go

109

and what you need to do next. But obediently following the quest markers will undoubtedly cause you to miss out on all sorts of useful treasure, secret locations, and optional events. Basic game theory states that the best loot should always be placed in the most illogical and out of the way locations. As such, it's much more to your advantage to go everywhere EXCEPT the place you're supposed to be going. You never know when you might find a treasure chest down a blind alley, an elixir in someone's bathtub, or a potato loving sage in a cave atop a seemingly unclimbable cliff.

If your world features PTD, you can safely take your time to comb every nook and cranny searching for useful items and secrets. If not, then you'll have to limit your searching to a reasonable amount of time to ensure that the demon lord or such doesn't end up destroying the world while you're off fishing or winning cooking contests. At the very least, be sure to set aside some time to visit the most remote and hard to reach spots, as they're likely to contain the best items, hidden shops, and other secret events.

If you find yourself wondering why someone would fill their bathroom with valuable healing items, you clearly have not been playing enough video games.

12. Pwning a Video Game Fantasy World

Going for Platinum

While completing your main quest or adventure is all well and good, that's not quite enough to be called truly l33t. To reach that lofty height, you must also platinum or 100 percent the game. This involves going everywhere, obtaining every item, completing every quest, mastering every skill, and basically doing everything. While having a complete collection of every type of fish in existence, or filling out every entry in your bestiary probably won't really help you save the world, it will earn you a massive amount of bragging rights when comparing notes with your fellow summoned/reincarnated heroes. After all, what's the point of being l33t if you don't have a concrete way of rubbing it in everyone else's face?

Completely mastering a game world tends to take a considerable amount of time and patience, and may involve many dull and repetitive tasks. If PTD is not in effect, there's a very real chance that you simply won't have the time needed to reach platinum. Ideally, you can save the less vital and more time-consuming tasks until after you've completed your main quest and saved the world. Though you will need to be careful, as some worlds feature mandatory deportation (see Chapter 17), which can easily ruin your post-game plans if it catches you unaware.

If, in the end, you lack the time or patience to reach 100 percent completion, you can always resort to the classic standby technique used by self-proclaimed l33ts everywhere ... lie and say you did. This approach is completely and totally foolproof, and guaranteed to never, ever come back and bite you ... except when it does, in which case you'll be royally screwed. Being honest might not win you quite as many accolades, but it's always the safer approach.

≋ 13 ≋

Hopelessly Trying
to Stay Alive
in a Dark Fantasy World

If you've determined that you've arrived in a dark fantasy world ... you're screwed. While it could be said in nicer terms, it's best to just get it out there. You're probably going to die. And, if you don't, you'll almost certainly end up wishing that you had. Dark fantasy worlds are violent, cruel, and unforgiving. While they do occasionally contain tiny rays of light and hope, said rays are usually only there to make your despair all the greater when they're brutally crushed before your eyes. That said, survival and escape aren't entirely impossible. The odds will be extremely stacked against you, but with the right approach and a massive amount of luck, you might have a tiny chance of pulling it off.

Immediate Survival

Other types of fantasy worlds like to start slow and build up, allowing new heroes the chance to get acclimated and learn the ropes before things get too dangerous. Dark fantasy worlds, on the other hand, tend to throw new arrivals off the deep end ... into a pit ... with spikes ... and sharks ... and spiky sharks ... with both hands and feet tied behind their backs. Also, the pit is full of lava. If you can manage to make it through your first couple of days without dying or losing your sanity, you'll be off to an excellent start. So heed our every warning and you might survive.*

---

* So You've Guides makes no promises of survival in dark fantasy worlds, and will accept no liability for any would-be heroes who or are maimed, killed, tortured, abused, assaulted, mentally devastated, or otherwise f***'d up despite, or even as a result of, following this guide.

Welcome to the dark side of the fantasyverse! Watch out for that first step, it's a doozie.

Getting the Hell Out of Gaeabrande

The best way, by far, to survive a dark fantasy world ... is not to be in a dark fantasy world. If you're very quick on the uptake, there's a slim chance that you can leave the world behind before it has a chance to destroy you.

If you arrived via portal, and you have even the tiniest suspicion that you might be in a dark fantasy world, immediately turn and run back through the portal as if your life depends on it (which it very much does). Upon arriving back on Earth, promptly destroy the portal so not even a scrap remains. Or, if that's not possible, seal it up so securely that nothing could ever get in or out of it again. And then move to the other side of the planet, just to be safe.

If you were summoned, reborn, or reincarnated, immediately fall to your knees and beg the gods, your summoner, or any other related powers to send you home. Or, at least to a different world. If successful, thank them profusely, then run away to some place where they'll hopefully never find you again.

Of course, dark fantasy worlds are rarely nice enough to let you escape so easily. More than likely, your portal will be closed, your summoner will turn a deaf ear to your pleas, and, seeing as the gods already hated you enough to send you to a dark fantasy world in the first place, they'll be uninclined to come to your aid. Still, it never hurts to try.

If escape isn't an immediate option, you can always keep it on the table as a long-term goal. You can learn more about possible escape routes in Chapter 18, though your odds of surviving long enough to reach any of them are abysmally low so, for now, it's best to focus all your energy on surviving, and put escape on the backburner until you've gotten a better handle on how to stay alive and sane.

Be Careful. Be Cautious. Be Overly Cautious.

You can safely assume that everyone and everything in a dark fantasy world is out to get you. Be it person, monster, plant, or even inanimate object, you're never safe. Let your guard down for even a moment, and you'll be beaten and robbed of everything you own. But that's only if you're "lucky." The less fortunate may be killed, or suffer a seemingly endless stream of fates worse than death. Torture, assault, mental torment.... Imagine the worst, most painful, most horrifying, and most depraved situation you can think of, and then multiply it by ten.

Naturally, you want to avoid any of that, and the best way to do so is with an overabundance of caution. Trust no one. Take every precaution. Always assume the absolute worst possible situation. Never expect an easy victory, even against a truly weak opponent. Don't think that your enemies are dead until you've destroyed their bodies down to the last atom (and even then, watch your back). Be ready for every boss to have a more powerful second form, followed by an even more powerful third form (and possibly a fourth and fifth after that). Never, ever believe for even a moment that you're safe, no matter how hidden, holy, or well defended your location is.

   People may call you paranoid, but that paranoia is the only thing protecting you against the countless unseen horrors that lurk around every corner. Don't let up, don't relax, don't stop doubting and suspecting everyone and everything. Maybe, just maybe, it will be enough to keep you alive for a little bit longer.

Think this guy looks tough? You haven't even seen 17.9532 percent of his full power.

Be Good, but Not Too Good

Morality in dark fantasy worlds is a tricky subject. While the fantasyverse normally loves a kind, sincere, good-hearted hero, those are exactly the type of people that dark fantasy worlds love to break or brutally murder in order to earn their "darker and edgier" credentials. At first glance, playing the truly irredeemable evil villain may seem like a better strategy to ensure your place in such a dismal world. And, in fact, that might work for a time. However, evil villains are still evil villains, no matter the world. While dark fantasy worlds do tend to give them some notable advantages, they're still sure to meet a horrible end eventually. And, if you try to perform a face-heel turn just to ensure your own survival, that end will probably come sooner rather than later.

Your best chance at survival is to adopt the persona of a dark, brooding, and violent anti-hero. Make sure to fight evil, but do it in as cold and cruel of a way as possible. Dress in dark clothes and carry lots and lots of weapons (overly large swords and anything with spikes are preferred). Violently dispatch your foes while ignoring their cries for mercy. Periodically take a moment after battle to mutter something about darkness and despair. Help others, but only when there's something in it for you. And never, ever grow too attached to your acquaintances or companions since they're almost certain to die sooner or later.

If you can't bring yourself to become that kind of person, you can simply wait and let things progress naturally. Any summoned or reincarnated hero who survives long enough in a dark fantasy world will end up becoming an anti-hero sooner or later as a result of countless failures and betrayals. However, if you take on that role from the beginning, it will not only increase your early chances of survival, it will also allow you to skip the mind-breaking traumatic events that are normally necessary to shape a dark fantasy hero (don't worry about missing out, you'll encounter plenty of other traumatic events later on).

Don't Let It Break You

You can't spend any length of time in a dark fantasy world without being damaged. So long as you remain, you will be hurt. You will be tortured and abused, both physically and mentally. Those around you will be tortured, abused, and killed by men and monsters while you watch helplessly. Tentacled beings of pure darkness and malice will tear open cracks in reality, and turn the world around you into a living hellscape filled with giant, naked, cannibal babies. Each and every day will bring new horrors and depravities.

In such situations, it's easy to lose your sanity. Dark fantasy worlds have a penchant for driving their inhabitants, hero and villain alike, to madness. But no matter what you see or what you suffer, you can't let it break you. Not completely. Taking on a cold and uncaring attitude can help, as can throwing away your morals and beliefs. Allow yourself to wallow in anger, hatred, and despair. Or simply go numb to all of it. Either approach will make you a better anti-hero and more likely to survive.

Of course, it might seem easier to merely give in and embrace the madness and the darkness. It might even be comforting. But that approach is certain to end in disaster. Sanity, once lost, is near impossible to regain and, unlike in other types of fantasy worlds, those taken by darkness can never return to the light. If you break, it's only a matter of time before you'll be claimed by death, or something much worse. But so long as you remain alive and unbroken, there's always a chance, however small, of victory or escape.

Slightly Longer–Term Survival

If you've managed to survive the initial gauntlet of violence and horrors that followed your arrival, then it's time to start thinking about your future (as little of it as there may be). If escaping to another world is off the table, you'll instead need to focus on completing your quest, which will hopefully make the world, as a whole, a bit less dark and deadly in the process. But, of course, the world won't make it easy for you.

Be Perfectly Prepared

If you've properly cultivated a strong sense of caution, your next step is to prepare yourself for any possible situation, no matter how far-fetched or unexpected. To a certain extent, you may be able to bluff and power your way through with a mixture of strength and general badassery, but that will only go so far. To better ensure your survival, you need a plan. And a backup plan. And a backup for the backup. Add in another dozen or so levels of backups and you might be good to go.

For example, it may seem unlikely that you'll randomly collapse from an undiagnosed illness mid-battle, that your opponent will effortlessly shrug off a nuclear blast, or that the demon lord will have a 1-Up handy, but in the off-chance that the demon lord uses his 1-Up to survive a nuclear bomb just as you collapse from a debilitating case of gas, you'll certainly be glad that you had the foresight to prepare a countermeasure. Is a zombie army advancing? Naturally you'll want plenty of holy water and blessed weapons, but you should also bring a collection of cursed gear as well, just in case these zombies have had their weaknesses reversed. For that matter, you should also have a plan in case the battle is interrupted by a platoon of dragons or a meteor strike. You should even have a plan ready in case you need to switch sides and lead the zombies against your former allies.

It might seem like overkill, but dark fantasy worlds love to throw major twists at you whenever your adventures seem to be going even a little bit too smoothly, so such extreme levels of preparation might actually end up being the bare minimum needed to survive.

Live and Let Die

At times, you may be tempted to spare a defeated enemy. In regular fantasy worlds, while there are risks, such an act could result in you gaining valuable information, or even a new ally. It can also raise your standing in the eyes of your party members. In a dark fantasy world, however, it's sure to backfire on you in the worst possible way. Most likely, your not-quite-fallen foe will take advantage of the temporary reprieve to recover and kill you or your love interest. Alternately, if the villain is only one step away from completing his evil plan or ritual, you can be certain that your misguided moment of mercy is all the time he needs to plunge the world into darkness.

The only reason you could conceivably have to keep a defeated enemy alive, is so you can torture him for information. And even then, he'll probably escape and return to royally screw you over later on. Remember, this is a dark fantasy world, not shonen manga land. The only good enemy is a dead enemy (at least until he rises up as an undead).

Rage Against the Heavens

Deities hold an odd place in dark fantasy worlds. At best, they're benevolent but, for some reason or other, powerless to stop the forces of darkness from twisting and destroying the world. In fact, the gods may have summoned you specifically to do what they can't. Or perhaps they're just lazy, apathetic, or went on a long vacation and haven't bothered to check their voicemail. As depressing as those scenarios sound, they're actually the best possibilities. Even if you can't count on the world's gods to help you out, at least they won't actively screw you over either.

Unfortunately, it's far more likely that the gods presiding over a dark fantasy world are just as evil and sadistic as any monster or demon. Or maybe they're not even proper "gods" at all, but some type of eldritch abominations that feed off of fear and suffering, driving men mad by their very existence. In such situations, it won't matter how many villains you defeat or goblins you slaughter, the world simply won't get any better unless you bring down the gods themselves.

Of course, such a feat is far easier said than done. If you're lucky, the so-called "gods" may be nothing more than extremely powerful immortal beings masquerading as deities. While their power is immense, they can be killed by a suitably powerful hero. Though you may need to catch them off guard, or use a special weapon, spell, or ritual to weaken them first. A true god, however, may very well be omniscient, omnipresent, and/or completely and totally invincible, making him impossible to defeat in any sort of fair fight. Meanwhile, the eldritch abomination type of "god," though theoretically killable, is so powerful and so contrary to the laws of reality that any attempt to face it will almost certainly only make things worse.

While going against a god that truly can't be killed might seem impossible, there could be other options. With the right magic tools or rituals, you may be able to seal away the god's power, or even the god himself. If the god is from another universe or dimension (as eldritch abominations typically are), you can try cutting off the method it uses to access your world. Sure, it might come back eventually, but that'll be a problem for some other hero centuries later, not something you need to worry about.

Unsurprisingly, the most difficult gods to defeat are those of the omniscient variety. Being all-knowing, they'll never be tricked, trapped, or destroyed. At least so long as they're paying attention and taking things seriously. You might be able to use their own carelessness or arrogance to bring about their downfall but, if that doesn't seem likely to work, the only other option is to find some way to block their omniscience (hats made of aluminum foil are the preferred method of crazy people everywhere, though their effectiveness varies). Of course, a smart and alert god will notice what you're doing and vaporize you long before you find said method (if it even exists). Remember, this is a dark fantasy world. Sometimes, there's simply no way you can win.

Don't Become the Next Dark Lord

If, against all odds, you actually manage to survive a dark fantasy world, complete your adventure, and depose whatever twisted gods or demons were using the world as their plaything, you'll likely find that you've become the most powerful being alive (or undead, as the case may be). At that point, you could try to return home, or settle down to a quiet life in what should now be a much less dangerous world. Or, assuming that your victory didn't leave you completely broken in mind and body, you may find yourself thinking that you could rule the world far better than its previous masters ever could. And, with your powers, there will be no one who can stop you from taking up the mantle of the former king, dark lord, or god. But no one survives a dark fantasy world unscathed, not even a victorious hero. By the end of your journey, you'll have spent so much time gazing into the abyss that it has probably moved far beyond gazing back, and has decided to possess you outright. Even with their gods sealed or destroyed, dark fantasy worlds are loath to lose their "darker and edgier" reputation, and will fight the change with everything they have. Corrupting the former hero into a new dark lord is one of their favored techniques. If you don't guard against it, you could easily find that everything you did on your journey was for naught.

A good first step is to simply turn down, or otherwise avoid, any position of power and authority, while doing your best to live a normal life. Of course, that's only a temporary measure, as the world isn't going to let you fade into obscurity so easily. Some find that making friends or starting a family helps keep them content and sane. This is especially true if your friends and/or love interest are former party members who managed to survive your adventures. Though, when they're later killed (which is an unfortunately common occurrence), it can easily push you over the brink. For that reason, others prefer to live a life of isolation, hidden away in some forgotten corner of the world, though even that method is hardly foolproof. In the end, what matters most is the mental fortitude and resilience to resist the urge for power and destruction no matter what happens.

Of course, you could always just give in and become that which you once hated. But, while being an evil despot might actually be fun for a while, it never pays off in the long run. Aside from the inherent moral issues, it's guaranteed that you'll die a miserable death at the hands of a future hero, and be dragged down to hell. In fact, if you truly find yourself succumbing to the darkness, it might be better to end things on your own terms before you lose yourself completely. Not a pleasant thought, but at least your legacy will remain intact. And hey, if you do end up in hell, you can always give a go at conquering it instead, an endeavor which offers all the violence and depravity of conquering the mortal world, with none of the guilt. If you decide to give it a try, big f'ing guns are known to be particularly effective.

≋ 14 ≋

Otherworldly Romance

If you're single (and, to be frank, nearly everyone who gets whisked off to a fantasy world is), you'll have plenty of chances to change that over the course of your adventure. In fact, don't be surprised if you end up inundated by attractive guys or girls vying for your affections. But, even though the fantasyverse generally supports its heroes' love lives as much as possible, there are still some issues and potential pitfalls of which you should be aware before you get swept away by a fantasy romance.

Identifying Your Options

Some of the more common options for potential romantic partners have already been listed in Chapter 9. Of those, the ones you're most likely to end up with are the troubled hottie, haughty noble, mysterious girl (if you're a guy), or the jerk with a heart of gold (if you're a girl). But really, any party member of the appropriate gender can be an option if you play your cards right. That said, there's no reason to limit yourself to your party members. Friendly guild employees, bartenders, waitresses, store clerks, and other people that you regularly encounter can all be added to the list if they fit your criteria. You'll also have a better than average chance with any unmarried, non-evil nobles that you happen to meet. Even attractive members of the evil emperor or demon lord's forces are fair game, especially if it appears that they're being tricked or coerced into service. Though, as a fair warning, romance with someone in the enemy camp has a much higher chance of ending in tragedy.

Now, that might seem like a very long list, but that's just the way the fantasyverse works. As detailed in their current collective bargaining agreement, all unmarried fantasy heroes are entitled to encounter no less than two attractive potential romantic partners during the course of their adventures, with a suggested average of four to six when available. While you're certainly free to try and romance all of them in order to create your own harem (more on that later), it's often much simpler to choose one lucky girl or guy to be your lover. But, seeing as you'll have multiple choices, don't be too quick to fall for the first pretty face, or even the first confession of love. Take it slow, weigh your options, and spend a while building up your relationships so you're absolutely sure that you'll be happy before committing.

Winning the Girl/Guy/Lizard Creature of Your Dreams

For native fantasy world heroes, winning the hearts of their beloveds is often a long and difficult process filled with countless setbacks and challenges. Earthly heroes, however, have it much easier. Considerable time and effort have been spent researching how summoned and reincarnated heroes, the majority of which lack any notable romantic history or skills prior to their trip to the fantasyverse, almost always amass a small army of would-be girlfriends or boyfriends almost immediately upon arrival. Recently, scientists have discovered the existence of isekaenol, a special pheromone that is only present in people who have traveled from Earth to the fantasyverse. Isekaenol is released automatically from the moment the hero arrives in a fantasy world, and triggers feelings of love and/or physical attraction in every potential romantic partner that he or she meets. The strength of its effects varies between individuals. In the most extreme cases, heroes have had to literally beat off their overly aggressive suitors with a stick to avoid being thrown into the nearest bedroom. But generally, the symptoms triggered by isekaenol initially manifest at a level somewhere between shy admiration and blatant flirting.

It should also be noted that the effects of isekaenol aren't necessarily limited to those of the opposite gender. This is especially likely in the case of female heroes (even more so when magically induced gender swaps are involved), who often find themselves attracting nearly equal amounts of suitors of both genders. If you think that sounds like fun, then you can simply sit back and enjoy all the extra attention. Unfortunately, isekaenol doesn't take your personal preferences into account so,

Regardless of your romantic history on Earth, after arriving in a fantasy world you're likely to find yourself quite popular. Perhaps too popular...

if you don't find the prospect very appealing, there's nothing you can do except politely discourage unwanted suitors and avoid any sort of shared bathing or swimming facilities at all costs.

While the power of isekaenol can easily attract the interest of your crush, it's rarely enough to seal the deal. (Unless you're dealing with a flaming pervert, in which case you should seriously reconsider your options ... or not? So You've Guides is here to give advice, not judge you for your questionable tastes.) Taking the time to get to know your chosen partner, flirting, giving gifts, and other standard dating practices will all help raise his or her affection. But, since you're in a fantasy world, you can also take advantage of additional tactics that are rarely available on Earth, such as saving your boyfriend or girlfriend's life in battle, performing assorted heroic deeds, and saving the world, all of which tend to result in large increases in affection. If, on the other hand, you're one of the unfortunate people who are extremely bad at interpersonal relations and constantly find yourself doing or saying the wrong thing, don't worry too much. Your relationships might progress a bit slowly but, thanks to the continued influence of isekaenol, it's nearly impossible to permanently damage your relationship with a potential love interest unless you do something truly cruel or depraved (which will also lead to an extremely nasty karmic reprisal down the road).

With all that in mind, getting your relationship to the stage of shy glances, frequent flirting, and a constant level of will-we-won't-we tension is typically very easy. However, many fantasy world relationships tend to hit a wall at this semi-final level, and pushing past it to obtain a clearly defined romantic relationship can be rather difficult. Most often, the key is to help your would-be lover overcome his or her greatest trial. This could be in the form of a family issue or past trauma, but most likely involves defeating a particular villain or monster, finding a certain treasure, or restoring the fortune and reputation of a fallen clan or kingdom. This is especially likely in the case of troubled hotties, mysterious girls, and jerks with a heart of gold.

However, if all of that sounds like too much work, there's a very good chance you can skip it all and jump straight to the romance by taking one easy step. Simply confess your feelings and ask the lucky guy or girl to go out with you. This approach is so rare and unheard of in the fantasyverse that the sheer shock of it triggers an enormous release of isekaenol, which will most likely catch your target completely off-guard and lead to an immediate and whole-hearted acceptance.* All you need to do is stop being a wuss and actually say something. If that seems too difficult, alcohol and post-battle highs have been known to serve as temporary confidence boosters.

Special note should be taken in regard to comic fantasy worlds. While it's guaranteed that you and your intended partner will end up in lots of sexy situations full of fanservice and accidental groping (regardless of gender), achieving an actual romantic and physical relationship can often seem near impossible. It's a well-established rule of comedy that massive amounts of unfulfilled sexual tension between two would-be lovers generates far more laughs than a stable relationship. As such, the world will do its best to keep the two of you right on the cusp but, just when it seems like you're about to make real progress, some sort of fanservice gag or unfortunate misunderstanding will pop up, often with results that are highly embarrassing and/or painful. Even

---

* Fantasyverse Surgeon General's Warning: Sudden confessions made by male heroes to female love interests have been known to trigger violent reflexive actions including, but not limited to slaps, punches, and fireballs. This is especially prominent in love interests suffering from extreme cases of shyness and/or tsundere syndrome. Please confess with caution.

a heartfelt confession is likely to be misheard or taken as a joke. In this situation, your only real option is to persevere. Be as forthright, sincere, and romantic as possible, and use your genre-savviness to try and avoid or mitigate mood ruining gags. If you stick with it, real progress should be made eventually, especially as you near the end of your adventure.

How to Keep Your Love from Dying in Your Arms

Even if you've yet to reach the final stage of your relationship, the very fact that someone is the object of your affection is enough to drastically reduce the odds of his or her survival. (Note that this only applies to heroes. If you ended up in a supporting or side role [see Chapter 5], you probably have nothing to worry about.) If your lover has a tragic past of some kind, you can expect it to return with a deadly vengeance. Otherwise, it will only be a matter of time before some villain sets his sights on your boyfriend/girlfriend in an attempt to break you. And, of course, there's always the pointlessly cruel death in battle.

In a comic fantasy world, you can avoid this so long as you prevent the world from falling victim to sudden bouts of drama (see Chapter 11). While in a dark fantasy world, it's pretty much unavoidable that your lover will either die or suffer a fate worse than death, so it's best not to get too attached from the beginning (or just do everyone else a favor and avoid romance entirely). In standard and video game fantasy worlds, however, there are some clear steps you can take to help ensure that the two of you will have your happily ever after.

- Train Regularly
  - Both you and your partner should be skilled in combat and keep up with training and/or leveling up. Nothing helps stave off death like some extra HP and DEF.
- Gear Up
  - A good set of armor or other defensive equipment makes a very practical (if not especially romantic) present.
- Stay Together
  - Solo missions are the perfect time for your lover to get kidnapped or mortally wounded.
- Stock Up
  - You really don't want to be that guy who let his girlfriend die because he forgot to carry around a healing potion.

- Have a Plan
  - Sooner or later your partner will be kidnapped or taken hostage (there's really no avoiding it), so make a plan of action for when that occurs.
- Beware Dangerous Foes
  - 42.3 percent of all doomed love interests are killed by either the big bad (the evil emperor, demon lord, etc.) or a villain from their past. Exercise extreme caution when facing any of these foes.
- Watch Your Back
  - 36.5 percent of all doomed love interests suffer a mortal wound when taking an attack meant for the hero. If you're never in mortal danger, you can eliminate this risk entirely.
- Don't Date Traitors
  - 7.71 percent of all doomed love interests die at the hands of the hero (often intentionally) after revealing their true loyalties. If you closely follow the information in Chapters 9 and 10, you should be able remove any spies or other traitors before they can worm their way into your heart.
- Make Sure It's Dead
  - Just because you defeated the big bad monster or evil minister or whoever, doesn't mean that he's totally dead. Enemies love to play possum, only to jump up and kill someone (probably your lover) once you've dropped your guard. So, after winning a fight, go ahead and decapitate, incinerate, or bury the bodies before they have a chance to recover. Actually, go ahead and do all three. Never hurts to be extra cautious.
- Remember the Magic
  - In many fantasy worlds, there exists some type of item, spell, or the like capable of reviving the dead; 5.089 percent of doomed love interests stay dead because all of their companions randomly forgot this fact.

Triggering the Harem Route

Why have one boyfriend or girlfriend when you could have two? Or three? Or nineteen? For some, the prospect of juggling that many relationships may sound horrifying. For others, it would be a dream come

Helpful reminder: In much of the fantasyverse, healing and revival magic is totally a thing.

true. Thanks to isekaenol, you're guaranteed to attract the attention of multiple potential partners during your stay in a fantasy world. While common sense would indicate that you should choose one of them, common sense essentially flew out the window when you ended up in a world of monsters, magic, and cat girls. So, if you're determined to have your own harem of sexy girls, hot guys, or even belligerent demons, that option actually might be on the table.

As a general note, you'll have the easiest time building up a harem in a comic fantasy world. Though, as previously discussed, pushing your relationships with its members into the final phase could be maddeningly difficult. Harems in dark fantasy worlds, meanwhile, are best avoided (like romantic relationships in general) unless you end up becoming a dark lord and use copious amounts of mind control. Though the chance that one of the members will eventually break free and kill you is rather high, so it isn't recommended.

Dark fantasy worlds aside, keep in mind that, no matter how strong their affection, not all of your love interests will necessarily be open to the idea of an actual harem. They may instead prefer to engage in an endless back and forth battle for your affections with no clear winner or loser ever surfacing. Your odds of getting them all onboard increase significantly if polygamy is already an established facet of the local culture. Of course, you don't actually have to marry the members of your harem, but it's generally expected that you'll do so sooner or later (the fantasy-verse is rather old fashioned that way). Note that, even if you haven't actually encountered anyone with multiple wives or husbands, that doesn't necessarily mean that polygamy isn't allowed. In some worlds, it's limited to people of a certain social or economic standing (such as royalty). In others, it may have fallen out of practice but is still considered a perfectly valid type of relationship. In addition, if you can create a strong feeling of friendship and familial affection between your love interests, or just convince them that you're too much man or woman for any one of them to handle, battling for your affection will start to lose its appeal in favor of a more cooperative approach.

Just remember, managing a harem requires far more time and effort than a traditional relationship. A neglected lover, or three, could easily change your personal paradise into a frigid hell. Even in comic fantasy worlds, keeping on top of your harem is a delicate balancing act, so be sure to carefully weigh the risks and rewards before attempting to take this route.

≈ 15 ≈

Kingdom Building 101

In the past, it was often enough for a summoned or reincarnated hero to defeat the evil whatever and save the world. But these days, fantasy worlds are demanding more of their champions. Saving the world is certainly still a key part, but you may also be called on to cook pots and pots of curry, start a successful business, solve clever puzzles, heal family relationships, or introduce the world to the wonders of mayonnaise (as a food or an instrument). But, by far, the most common additional task that summoned heroes are asked to perform is that of building and leading your very own kingdom. In such cases, having a nation that is strong and successful economically and militarily at your back will be vital to both your own survival, and that of the world as a whole.

Everybody Wants to Rule the World

While many dream of being the man or woman in charge, few actually have the knowledge or skills necessary to pull it off. It's quite easy to become a petty tyrant or a weak, ineffectual leader. To put it bluntly, not everyone is leadership material, and that might include you. Fortunately, you can always make use of the powerful and time-honored tradition known as "faking it." The easiest way to do this is to pull from Earth's rich history of war, governance, and nation building. While fantasy worlds have their own long and rich history for you to learn (or ignore, as it's often not all that important), there are sure to be a number of governmental techniques and military strategies from Earth that will completely and utterly revolutionize everything the locals have ever known about leading a nation. Earth is just that much better (or worse, depending on how you look at it). You *were* paying attention in history class, right? Fortunately, even if you don't know Napoleon from Neapolitan, or you think that Julius Caesar invented a salad dressing, you can make up for your poor studying habits by planning ahead and bringing along a large collection of eBooks on history, governance, economics, and the like to shore up your knowledge (see Chapter 2). That said, since your ability to bring physical objects with you from Earth isn't guaranteed, it's far better to actually learn all of that stuff in the first place.

Once you have the knowledge, how do you actually get put in charge of your own kingdom or empire? In many cases, the current king, queen, ministers, or the like will automatically appoint you as such due to your status as an otherworldly hero. This is especially true in nations that are already, for one reason or another, on the brink of collapse. In some cases, this might necessitate marrying into the existing royal family. However, your new spouse is guaranteed to be kindhearted and highly attractive, the fantasyverse is just cool that way. He or she may be apprehensive at first, but will fall deeply in love with you within a short period of time thanks to a combination of isekaenol and your own innate charm. In addition, because royalty are typically allowed harems of some sort, this forced marriage shouldn't impact your relationship with any other potential romantic partners.

If simply being a hero isn't enough to gain the crown, you may find that you have to conquer your new kingdom by force. While that may sound rather difficult to do on your own, it's actually not unheard of for an insanely overpowered hero to be able to defeat an entire army single-handedly. If you're not quite at that level, you can always take command of a local group of rebels to increase your fighting power. Or, if you'd prefer to limit casualties as much as possible, you can always attempt to simply depose or assassinate the current leader(s). Though, do note that unless said leaders are extremely unpopular, this approach is likely to cause considerable anger and unrest among the populace.

Finally, if there's no convenient kingdoms to take over, you could always build your own from scratch. All you really need is an empty plot of land and a group of people (human or not) willing to put you in charge. Roaming tribes, refugees, and intelligent monsters are all good choices. Just pop in, demonstrate your impressive leadership skills, overwhelming power, or some combination of the two, and you're good to go. Or, if you're rather lacking in one or both of those areas, just BS your way to the top. It's so easy, even a talking skeleton can do it! Of course, neighboring countries probably won't take kindly to a new nation popping up on their doorstep, so you'll need to be ready with some high-level diplomacy and/

Sometimes, all it really takes to become the king is the right outfit and a good speech. You'd also be surprised what a little bit of ballot fraud can do.

or an overwhelming show of force early on to make sure that your country survives long enough to get up and running.

Axes and Allies

No matter how overpowered you are, protecting and managing an entire kingdom is impossible to do on your own. As such, recruiting trustworthy allies to fill roles in both the military and domestic fields is an absolutely vital step in the building of any successful kingdom. Do note that these allies will not necessarily overlap with your party members. A top-notch accountant is a godsend (sometimes literally) for any nation, even if he's the only person in your cabinet who is unable to curb stomp a dragon. While there will often be dozens of positions that you need to fill to keep your country running smoothly, the following are the most critical.

- Steward/Chamberlin
  - The steward's job is to handle all the nitty gritty nuts and bolts

of running a kingdom. He must be highly knowledgeable about law, customs, and the current geopolitical climate, while also being an expert in time management. It's his tireless (and often thankless) work which allows an inexperienced hero to be a successful monarch. If you're lucky, such a figure will already be in place upon your ascension to leadership. Otherwise, you'll need to quickly make every effort to recruit a suitable candidate. A word of warning, despite his high rank and importance, try to avoid making your steward the official second-in-command, as doing so will drastically increase the odds of betrayal somewhere down the line.

- Accountant/Treasurer
  - While you might think that buying the latest weapons and armor for your party is expensive, that's small change compared to what's required to keep a kingdom up and running. And while collecting taxes and tariffs, making payments, and balancing the books is a herculean challenge, most heroes would much rather risk life and limb against deadly monsters than spend their days wrangling with a stack of expense reports.
- Head Maid
  - As king or queen, you've got far more important things to do with your time than basic housework, especially if you're living in a palace. Only a truly special individual can command the small army of maids and other staff necessary to maintain a royal residence. She'll also ensure that you're dressed appropriately for any occasion, remember to eat properly, and get enough sleep. Most importantly, as maids often become potential romantic interests, you should choose one with a suitable personality (lovingly demure, playfully flirty, and coolly demeaning are all popular choices) and ensure she's supplied with a proper frilly black and white dress.
- Bodyguard
  - It's bad enough when every single monster, villain, and random thug is out to get you. But, as a ruler, you'll also have to deal with assassins and political rivals both at home and abroad. Assuming you've been keeping up with your training, you should be able to handle most threats on your own, but an extra layer of protection never hurts. A strong bodyguard can

also protect you when you're sleeping, ill, or just feeling really lazy. While strength and skill are the key elements of a good bodyguard, feel free to choose an attractive member of the opposite sex if you want to add a bit of extra romantic tension to your daily routine.

- Spy Master
  - Information can be far deadlier than any weapon, and no kingdom will survive long without someone skilled in its use and acquisition. Some rely on stealth, others on an extensive network of informants. Ninja gear and an army of shadow doppelgangers are optional but highly recommended.
- Military Leader
  - Unless you're an expert on battlefield tactics, you'll need someone to oversee the command and strategy for your army during battle. Even if you do have the big picture under control, you'll want trusty sub-commanders to ensure that every maneuver is properly carried out. This is especially true when forced to fight on multiple fronts. Don't be tempted to try and handle everything yourself, no matter how powerful you are. A one-man army may be enough to win a battle, but rarely an entire war.
- Trainer
  - Do you want to scream yourself hoarse day in and day out while molding a bunch of raw recruits into a world-class fighting force? (Or, at least getting them to the point where they won't stab themselves in the foot every time they try to sheath their swords.) No? Well, that's why you need someone to do it for you.
- City Planner
  - Setting up zoning regulations, managing traffic flow, maintaining water and sewage systems, upholding law and order…. A talented city planner can do it all, with the bare minimum number of giant lizard attacks.

Finally, don't stop once you've filled the above positions. Any sufficiently talented individuals can become huge assets to your kingdom if you find the right way to use them. Got a good singer? Start an idol troop to bring in additional fame and revenue. A world-renowned gourmand? Have him tell you about unusual dishes and ingredients that can be used to reduce food shortages. A top-notch gambler? Challenge your neighboring kingdoms to a few "friendly" bets. A half-human spider monster with a bad case of multiple personality disorder? Eh, you're bound to think of something eventually. Just be creative and never let any talented individual slip through your fingers.

Jumpstarting the Industrial Revolution

If you're going to all the trouble of running your own kingdom, you might as well upgrade it with some of the comforts of home. While there are notable exceptions, the vast majority of fantasy worlds are stuck firmly in medieval times, perhaps with magic being used to provide a handful of more modern comforts. Trying to jump straight to the modern era probably won't work, but there's no reason you can't give your kingdom a nudge in the right direction, especially with regard to creations that will enhance daily life and national defense. With your knowledge of Earth's SCIENCE (or at least some good eBooks on how things are made), and enough time and effort, you can create guns, telephones, air conditioners, or even motorcycles.

First, you need to decide on what specific technologies you want to introduce. Remember that some items have prerequisites of sorts. For example, you may not be able to create a combustion engine without first introducing improved forms of metallurgy. You also need to beware of any technology that would be dangerous in the wrong hands (such as bombs), since you probably won't be able to maintain a monopoly on it for long. Next, you need skilled craftsmen who can turn your designs into reality. Depending on your goals, and the level of technology already present in the world, this process could be fairly quick and simple, or a lengthy undertaking which involves significant trial and error.

You may also be able to use magic to substitute for various components such as powering your plumbing system with water magic, or using lightning spells in place of an electric generator. Don't be afraid to think outside the box of Earthly science and physics and enter the realm of magitech. With careful planning and enough time and effort, you may create a marvelous civilization surpassing even that of Earth … or you might create a giant spider mech that goes out of control and destroys everything. While technology is great, sometimes it's better to just be happy with what you have, or at least remember to always install an off-switch.

Command and Conquer

In a fantasy world, a kingdom never goes for any significant length of time without a war of some sort. Yours will naturally be no exception. Whether from a demon lord, evil empire, or a jealous neighbor who wants to steal your farmland, it's really only a matter of time before hostilities start. You may be able to head some of them off with diplomacy. This is where your steward and spy master can really shine, providing all the information you need to convince your foes that they'd be far better off working with you, or perhaps under you, than against you. Treaties, bribes, "friendly" shows of force, and even political marriages can all factor in.

Of course, sometimes war is the only option. Once again, your knowledge from Earth can prove invaluable in regard to military strategy and tactics, though magic has a tendency to throw a wrench into things from time to time. Siege warfare, for example, falls to pieces when you can magically create food and water. Or, for that matter, simply teleport into the opposing monarch's bedroom. Other useful tactics include cutting your enemies down with magically focused rays of sunlight, creating a ridiculously large army of golems, and sacrificing the enemy forces to summon eldritch goat monsters.

If magic isn't your thing, and you managed to bring some modern military gear with you, you'll soon discover that most armies in the fantasyverse are woefully unprepared to face off against a machine gun or a tank. Wielding modern heavy weaponry could make your army truly unmatched on the field of battle ... at least until you run out of bullets and/or gas. And, once again, magic can easily serve as the great equalizer in some worlds, so beware sorcerers, magic beings, demi-gods, and cute girls wielding gigantic weapons.

On that note, if you do find your forces facing off against a young girl with an overly large weapon of any kind, just go ahead and surrender. It doesn't matter how big your army is, or what kind of strategy and weapons you're using, you're going to lose. If she's unknowingly aligned with the side of evil, you might be able to woo her to defect via seduction and/or really good food. If not, your only options are to either run away, or send your own cute weapon girl in response. As such, it's recommended to have at least several such girls in reserve at all times.

Once you've won the war, treat your conquered enemies strictly but fairly. Do your best to prevent the usual post-war looting and pillaging

If your enemies have a girl like this on their side, run.

that often characterizes medieval forces and, whenever possible, offer the hand of support and friendship to the defeated populace. Whether or not you plan to actually take over the defeated nation's territory for yourself, a little goodwill goes a long way towards preventing future conflicts, which you're sure to have more than enough of anyway.

≋ 16 ≋

How an Earthly Hero
Saved the World

You've survived the early challenges, formed a powerful party, trained, grown, laughed, loved, and maybe even founded a kingdom. But all of that was only to prepare you for the true purpose of your new fantasy world life. If you've made it this far, you may already have a solid idea of what your main quest entails, and the goals you need to accomplish in order to succeed. But let's take a moment to review and ensure that you're on the path to victory.

Although there are rare exceptions, a trip to the fantasyverse normally has some strings attached. Sooner or later, you'll be expected to save your new world (or at least a portion of it) from disaster. The nature of this disaster will vary but, in most cases, it involves the rise of an evil something (demon/monster/villain/empire/spider/brain-in-a-jar/etc.). Often, your goddess or summoner will fill you in on the details from the start. If you came through a portal or some other means, you can instead expect to learn all you need from a friendly local, or get mixed up in some sort of battle or other event that will allow you to quickly piece together the details. If none of the above has happened to you, just give it some time. While most heroes receive their main quest almost immediately, others have to wait days, months, or even years before the true purpose of their journey is made known. (That is almost certain to be the case if you were reborn in the body of a child, and need time to grow into your powers and out of your diapers.)

Once the evil whatever has been identified, your goal is clear. Go out, quest, travel, train, and finally defeat it. Straight up combat is the most common approach but, depending on your skills and the nature of the threat, you may instead have to obtain victory via diplomacy, military strategy, puzzle solving, or even dating (after all, even evil needs love). Once again, the specific method needed will generally be made clear early on. If not, it should be easy enough to infer based on the type of evil, and your own skill set. The entire process tends to be rather cut and dry, but we'll go over some of the specifics just in case you need a nudge in the right direction.

Unlocking Your True Power

During the latter portion of your adventure, it's quite common to encounter an enemy that you simply can't defeat, no matter how many levels you gain and how much new equipment you buy. But don't despair, you just need to unlock your true power!* (Unless you're in a dark fantasy world, in which case you're either screwed or just need to get horrendously tortured for a while first.) Every hero has an amazing power locked away inside, just waiting to be accessed at a suitably dramatic moment and turn the tides of battle back in your favor. Do note that, if you're already extremely overpowered, you may never find yourself in such a situation and any true power you have will remain unused and unnecessary.

There are many ways to unlock your true power. Sometimes, it requires undergoing strenuous (or just plain unusual) training, often from an eccentric old master who lives in the most inaccessible location in the entire world. Other times, you may need to confront and defeat your inner demons to gain the necessary mental strength and fortitude. (Note that, in the fantasyverse, the phrase "inner demons" is not always a metaphor.) Maybe your true power is simply a drama queen that's waiting for the last possible moment to awaken. The details often don't matter so much as the fact that you've done something, and/or ended up in a suitably hopeless situation. Once those conditions are met, your inner power should be unlocked and ready to be unleashed.

The most common way to unleash your inner power is by screaming yourself hoarse while striking some sort of suitably dramatic pose. If the initial explosion of raw force doesn't wipe out your enemies, your

---

* Fantasyverse Surgeon General's Warning: If suffering from an untreated case of inner darkness, unlocking your true power can result in overwhelming bouts of anger, aggression, and general evilness. If you begin exhibiting any of these symptoms, immediately seek aid from your nearest love interest.

massive boost in speed and power will. If screaming isn't really your thing, you can instead flash an evil grin while laughing at how foolish your enemies are to push you to this level (say, over 9,000). Tossing out a line about how you haven't even used half of your full power, or how this isn't even your final form never hurts either. After that, just go all out. It may take you some time to gain a complete mastery of your newly found powers, but you're guaranteed to be more than strong enough to annihilate your current foes.

The Final Battle

In the end, it all comes down to a final showdown between your party and the biggest, baddest, evilest creature in the world. Whether

Possible side-effects of unleashing your true power include: quick and effortless victory, awesome pyrotechnics, and a really sore throat.

a man, sexy sorceress, eldritch horror, or some sort of giant toad thing, don't let appearances fool you. This is by far the strongest and deadliest being you have ever faced. If you haven't already unlocked your true power, this is the time to do so. Also, feel free to use any secret moves, ultimate equipment, or other aces in the hole that you've been holding onto. Don't give your enemy time to attack, power-up, or even say hello. Just go in swords and spells blazing. If you're lucky and powerful enough, you might even take him out before he has the chance to do anything. A bit anti-climactic, sure. But considering that final bosses like to pull cheap moves like one-shotting your party members, killing your love interest before your eyes, and destroying the entire world out of spite, anti-climactic really isn't so bad. If you instead end up in a long, drawn-out battle, just do your best, keep getting up, and never say die (unless you're taunting your opponent). Assuming that you and your party have kept up with your training, equipment upgrades, and such, you should win eventually, though it may be by the skin of your teeth.

Even when it appears that you've won, don't get complacent. Final bosses often have multiple forms, each more powerful than the last (even if their looks suggest otherwise). Beware sudden power surges, mysterious rumbling, ominous laughter, magical chants, and sudden changes to the background music. Said bosses also love to play dead only to stab you in the back, or the front, or wherever they can reach, the moment you let your guard down, so keep attacking until they have been completely and utterly destroyed, body and spirit, before you even think about celebrating.

Alternate Victory Conditions

Strange though it may sound, there are actually a handful of fantasy worlds that aren't being threatened by some great evil. Instead, they may call on summoned heroes to fulfill other vital, if less exciting, roles. Once again, the nature of the problem being faced, and your expected role, will normally be made clear early on. In the case of worlds where you need to recover a lost treasure or rescue an important person, a large part of your quest will likely still revolve around defeating an evil something that also wants to steal the treasure or eliminate your VIP, so there's little practical difference. There are, however, a few possible victory conditions that are entirely unrelated.

Nation Building

While nation building is often undertaken in order to strengthen a country in preparation to fight an evil empire or the like, sometimes there's actually no real goal beyond the creation of a strong, thriving country. Without any looming threat on the horizon, you're free to focus all of your efforts on building the best country possible, whether that means developing a robust economy, creating a just and equal society, building up convenient modern infrastructure, or founding a strong royal lineage (royalty and harems tend to go hand-in-hand). While defense should never be neglected, you'll likely be able to solve most conflicts with other nations via trade and diplomacy. In cases like this, there may not actually be a specific "victory condition" beyond continually increasing the power and prosperity of your nation. Just keep working at it, don't become an evil emperor, and remember that it's good to be the king.

Self-Realization

In some worlds, the goal is more internal. While combat, nation building, puzzles, and the like might be involved to varying extents, they're all secondary. Instead, to truly succeed, you must learn to know and accept yourself (congratulations if you can do so without triggering some sort of human instrumentality apocalypse). This means coming to terms with your darkest secrets and biggest failings, and learning to grow and overcome them in order to become a better person. Without that growth, any other sort of victory you may achieve is meaningless, and will soon be undone by your own shortcomings.

For some, such a goal can be far more difficult than any battle. However, you can rest assured that, while it may not be the adventure you want, it's the adventure you need. And success is within your grasp, no matter how impossible it may seem. Worlds with quests of this type operate on a strict system of balance and karma, borrowing your power to deal with their own issues and then returning you to Earth as a better person than you were before. As to what issues you'll have to face, that naturally varies from person to person but, deep down inside, you probably already know. You can expect a wise, almost parental guide, understanding party members, and a whole lot of metaphors. Keep an open heart and mind, and never let go of your desire to grow and change, and you should do just fine.

Cooking

It's a little-known fact that 15.3 percent of all problems in the fantasyverse can be solved by really good food. As such, cooking makes for an extremely useful skill to pick up alongside your swordsmanship and magical abilities, and is sure to serve you well throughout any adventure. However, in some worlds, cooking isn't just the answer to a few problems, but to all the problems. Have you encountered an elven village suffering from malnourishment? Bake them a few pizzas. Are people transforming into demons? Just stuff some curry into their mouths (or a Snickers, if you have one). Did you run into a legendary monster? Woo it with some ginger beef and get a new pet. Need to turn your fledgling country into an economic powerhouse? Behold the power of mayonnaise!

Even if you weren't much of a chef back on Earth, in many worlds cooking is an official ability that you can learn and level up like any other. You'll have to sacrifice some skill points, but who needs healing magic or spear proficiency when you can make awesome teriyaki chicken (or cockatrice)? However, if you do have at least some basic knowledge of cooking, or remembered to download some cookbooks onto your cellphone before leaving Earth, you can quickly become a rising star in the culinary world by introducing popular foods from your former life. American and Japanese dishes in particular tend to be huge hits, and are sure to win the favor of not only your party members, but

Behold the power of curry!

local shopkeepers, adventurers, and even nobility. You might not have access to all the ingredients that you're used to, but it shouldn't be too hard to find plants and herbs with similar flavors. You'll also be surprised just how many monsters taste like chicken. A bit of creativity and experimentation can take you even further. Slimes, for example, can be made into surprisingly good noodles for some reason. Just roll up your sleeves, pull out your knife (or sword, if you prefer), and start cooking.

Beware the Last-Minute Plot Twist

Once you've finished your epic world-shaking battle (or cooking contest) and saved the country, world, universe, and whatever else there is to save from the greatest evil threat to ever exist (until the next one), it's finally time to rest and bask in your victory ... or maybe not. The fantasyverse loves last-minute plot twists. In fact, it would be more surprising if the final boss didn't rise from the dead (remember to destroy his body and spirit before he has the chance to do so), or activate some ultimate doomsday spell that you have to stop before he takes the world down with him. It's also possible that the being you thought was the ultimate evil was only the second-in-command (or worse, the middle manager) for something far, far more dangerous. In which case, you better hope that you still have some hidden power left to call upon. Or, if the fantasy world and villain are particularly unoriginal, you might only have to deal with escaping from a collapsing fortress.

There are many forms these sorts of plot twists can take, and they don't always make themselves known immediately. It might be hours, days, or even weeks before you realize just how much trouble you're really in. The best you can do is stay alert and focus your genre-savviness for signs of anything that might be amiss. Of course, if the world in question really wants to mess with you, there might be no twist at all, just lots of little hints to make you think that there will be. So be ready, but try not to turn yourself into a paranoid wreck in the process. After all, you did save the world (at least for now), and you deserve to enjoy the accolades, rewards, and, most importantly, the peaceful downtime that results.

➥ 17 ⬿

Now What?

At long last evil has been defeated (for the moment). The world is safe (relatively speaking). Any lingering personal issues have been overcome (or successfully ignored). And, you've gotten together with the guy or girl (or harem) of your dreams. So, what comes next? During the initial months, or perhaps years, of your fantasy world life, there was always the big quest driving you forward. The need to save the world, beat the game, expand your kingdom, catch all the monsters, or start a successful pizza chain. But once that goal has been fulfilled, many heroes find themselves unsure of how to approach the future. It's time to take a step back and ask, "how do you want to spend the rest of your life?"

Avoiding Mandatory Deportation

One thing to be wary of, or perhaps look forward to, is the mandatory deportation contract that some fantasy worlds foist upon Earthly heroes (talk to your goddess, summoner, or game designer for more information). Translated from fantasy legalese, it essentially states that any heroes brought from other worlds will, upon completion of their quest, be returned to the place from whence they came. The remaining details vary considerably by world, but there are several clauses you should pay particular attention to. (Note: If your world doesn't have a mandatory deportation contract [which is typically the case if you arrived via death or portal], feel free to skip to the next section. Alternately, if you lack a contract but really want to leave anyway, see Chapter 18.)

- The Clause of Remembrance
  - States whether or not you'll retain the memories of your

adventures after returning to Earth. This is generally allowed, unless the world is relatively easy to access and wants to avoid getting swarmed by tourists.

- The Clause of Magic and Abilities
  - Details which magic spells and abilities you've learned over the course of your adventure, if any, that will be retained upon returning to Earth. You'll likely be able to keep skills that already exist in both worlds, such as swordsmanship or cooking. However, things like teleportation, shapeshifting, summoning really cute bears, and any form of magic are unlikely to make the transition. If they do, you may find yourself becoming a superhero, or being hunted by a clan of rogue sorcerers upon your return. Fortunately, we have guides available for purchase to help you with those situations.
- The Clause of Assorted Stuff
  - Covers which of the items and equipment that you've collected, if any, will return to Earth along with you. At best, you can expect to keep whatever you're currently wearing and carrying at the time of deportation, so you may want to consider preparing a return home pack (much like your initial survival pack) that you keep on yourself at all times. Though, as a note, there is a significant chance that any magical items will fail to work when removed from their original world. There's also the very real risk that suddenly appearing in the middle of a modern city while carrying a sword or riding a dragon could get you arrested, or even killed by the local authorities (in general, dragons fair rather poorly against fighter jets). Alternately, you may end up being sent home entirely naked. While that is still likely to attract the attention of local authorities, the resulting fallout will be far more embarrassing than deadly.
- The Clause of Time Displacement
  - Specifies whether you'll be returned to the exact moment of time at which you left Earth, or if you'll arrive after going missing for as many months or years as you spent in the fantasyverse. Naturally, the former is generally far more convenient when it comes to smoothly resuming your original life. Though in extreme cases, it can lead to a confusing

Unlike in the fantasyverse, walking down an Earthly street while carrying a large sword is likely to cause a bit of a commotion.

mismatch between your physical and mental ages. But considering what some people would give to become young again, it's really a good deal.

- The Clause of Hopefully Not Getting Screwed Over
  - An addendum to the previous clause that deals with what happens if the fantasyverse attempts to return you to your original body and time right after you were killed on Earth. Ideally, you want to get a slight time rewind (so you can avoid your untimely demise), or a magic handwave (you totally

didn't get crushed by that truck after all). If not, it's quite possible that you could wind up horribly injured, or just plain dead on arrival. At worst, you might find yourself turning into an undead abomination and bringing about the zombie apocalypse. Be sure to read the fine print.

- The Clause of Not Getting Deported
  - Of course, you might not want to leave your new world at all. Maybe you died back home and the Clause of Hopefully Not Getting Screwed Over isn't doing you any favors. Maybe you don't want to leave your new harem. Maybe you really enjoy being a vending machine. Or maybe you'd rather live life as a young, attractive, heroic adventurer instead of an

The exact time and place that you appear when returning to Earth are very important.

overweight, thirty-something shut-in. In that case, you'll need to see if there's any way to opt out of deportation and continue enjoying your new life.

But what if there is no option to opt out? If you've got a benevolent goddess or summoner on your side, you can simply ask not to be returned to Earth. Assuming that the rules of magic don't somehow prevent it, there shouldn't be any issues since you are the hero that saved the world and all. In other situations, you'll need to find a loophole.

Perhaps the simplest way of avoiding mandatory deportation is to not complete your main quest or goal. Don't challenge the game's final dungeon. Leave the poor demon lord alone (after all, what did he ever do to you?). Let the legendary hidden treasure stay hidden. Forget about all of that and just enjoy your life. Of course, you'll be screwing over the rest of the world in the process (and may trigger a nasty karmic reprisal as a result), but if you're ok with that, it's a rather foolproof method. Just don't expect it to be easy. Whether via bad luck, karma, or divine intervention, fantasy worlds have lots of ways to try and force you back on task. You can expect to deal with loads of deus ex machina and angry locals determined to make you the hero, even if you need to be dragged all the way kicking and screaming. As such, most heroes find that this approach is unsustainable in the long run. Another tactic is to search for a loophole in the wording of the contract. Maybe you can "accidentally" show up late to the portal, or change your name so the spell doesn't recognize you. Creativity and genre-savviness can help you here.

Even if your contract is iron tight, you still may be able to get out of it by interfering with the magic spells that enforce the deportation. Magic dampeners, spell cancelers, and defensive spell forms are all worth trying. If you're not very magically inclined, you can ask one of your party members or other allies for assistance, assuming that person doesn't secretly (or not-so-secretly) want you gone. You could also attempt to overpower the spell by anchoring yourself strongly to the world through use of a binding spell, slave collar, or even the power of love and friendship.

While none of these approaches are 100 percent guaranteed, you've got a fairly good chance of staying in the fantasyverse if you try hard enough.

Livin' la Vida Fantasy

Once you're certain that you won't be undergoing an unwanted trip back to Earth, you're free to enjoy your fantasy world life to the fullest. There are no hard and fast rules about what you need to do after your adventures are finished. Chances are, you'll have amassed considerable power and/or wealth along the way, so there will be lots of options available. Some former heroes prefer to continue adventuring, traveling, fighting monsters, and living a life of exploration and excitement. Others "retire" to start a family and run a business. Popular choices include training academies, crafting workshops, and restaurants. Heroes whose quest had a strong focus on nation building will get to reap the rewards (and responsibilities) of the royal life. Alternately, if you managed to earn enough money (via combat or business acumen), you can just buy a giant mansion and lay around all day while being waited on by a troop of sexy maids or butlers. That option may not do much for your public image, but you've got a mansion, sexy servants, and a giant mountain of gold, so who cares about that?

Poor Life Choices

Just because the world was saved doesn't mean that you're entirely out of danger. Of course, that should be a given in a dark fantasy world where you're never, ever safe. But even worlds of other types can quickly turn on you if you make a mistake, bringing your post-adventure life to a sudden, and often violent end. To make sure you survive to enjoy your retirement to the fullest, avoid making the following poor fantasy life choices.

- Leaving Loose Ends
  - Was there some optional task that you left on the backburner while completing your main quest? Perhaps a person in need of help? A minor villain who escaped? An unsettling rumor floating about? Best to deal with all of those things sooner rather than later. In the fantasyverse, loose ends have a way of coming back to bite you in the ass (or kick you in the balls) if you let them fester for too long.
- Getting Cocky
  - Just because you defeated the eldritch incarnation of pure evil

150

doesn't make you invincible. There's usually some sleeping monster or ancient master out there that's stronger than you are. And, aside from video game worlds (where everything runs on stats), there's still the risk that some street punk or random monster could catch you off-guard with a cheap shot. So don't showboat, don't give your enemy a free attack, and never let your guard down in a situation that has the potential to become even remotely dangerous.

- Neglecting Your Training
  - Many heroes get a bit lazy after saving the world only to find that, when danger once again rears its ugly head, they're overweight, under-leveled (levels, like muscles, tend to atrophy when not used), out of practice, and can't remember where the heck they put their legendary equipment. Don't be one of those heroes. Train, stay in shape, and keep your best weapon and armor easily accessible at all times.
- Becoming a Tyrant
  - Being one of the strongest people in the world makes it easy to become drunk on power. Soon you start to think that you need more, you deserve more. And, for that matter, the world would be much better off if it catered to your whims. Whether your path is one of greed and debauchery, fire and blood, or well-intentioned extremism, you can be sure that, sooner or later, a new hero will rise up to overthrow you.
- Training a Future Hero
  - It's only natural for legendary heroes such as yourself to pass their skills on to the next generation. After all, you won't always be around to save the world (unless you became immortal during your journey, in which case you might). However, doing so automatically changes your official fantasyverse role ID from hero to some type of guide or mentor. Specifically, the type that almost always gets killed in order to motivate the new hero to begin his or her journey. It may mean leaving the world a bit unprepared, but it's much safer to let your skills die with you (preferably of old age). Though, there's also something truly satisfying about watching a promising youngster learn, grow, and maybe even surpass you, so some find it to be worth the risk. The choice is up to you.

Evil Never Dies

Fantasy worlds never stay saved for very long. If you're extremely lucky, you may end up with a few centuries of peace between major world-ending threats but, realistically, you're more likely to have somewhere between a few days and a few decades. And, as the hero who already saved the world once, it's no surprise that everyone will be looking to you to step up once again. Whether you're rejoined by your original party or a group of plucky new heroes, don't be surprised if you're actually called on to save the world two, three, or even a couple dozen times over the course of your life.

With a good information network and a penchant for early action, you can nip a number of upcoming threats in the bud before they reach "the fate of the world" level of danger. But, sooner or later, something will slip through the cracks, and you will have to face it. To increase your odds of survival, make sure to never stop training and growing stronger. Threats to the world operate on a linear scale, with their power increasing progressively each time. As such, you'll be lucky if the super-move you used to kill the last demon lord even scratches the next one. As previously mentioned, you should also think carefully before becoming a mentor to a younger hero, as that drastically increases your chance of death. Sure, your young protégée will avenge you, but you'd probably rather avoid getting stabbed through the heart in the first place. If you absolutely have to take on an apprentice, make sure to remind him or her that healing magic and items are totally a thing and, if you're ever mortally injured, said spells and items should be used immediately, before any screaming, crying, or swearing of revenge. That said, training a talented youngster is certainly the heroic thing to do, and there are some mentors that survive (especially the ones that take appropriate precautions), so it's worth considering if the opportunity presents itself.

≋ 18 ≋

Homeward Bound

Sometimes, it's just time to leave. Perhaps the fantasy life isn't all you dreamed it would be. Fantasy worlds might be fun, but they're also dangerous. Injury, disease, and killer death bunnies are ever-present threats. You might have family, or at least a pizza delivery, waiting for you back on Earth. Maybe you're scared. Or, it could be that the idea of spending the rest of your life in a world without TV and internet access is just too depressing to think about. When you seriously consider the logistics of adjusting to life in an entirely different world with a vastly different culture and level of technology, it's not hard to see why some heroes quickly become disillusioned. But what if your world lacks a mandatory deportation clause? Or if you just don't want to go to all the trouble of completing some big, dangerous, complicated quest in the first place? Fortunately, you aren't without options.

Identifying the Escape Routes

Most fantasy worlds have at least one or two ways to return to Earth, even without relying on a deportation clause. These possible "escape routes" tend to be quite predictable in nature depending on the type of world and how you arrived.

- If you arrived via portal:
  - Most portals allow passage back and forth between Earth and their designated world. However, it's not uncommon for the portal to only activate under certain conditions such as on a specific day of the week, in the presence of a special magic item, or when you click your heels together and sing about how much you want to go home. If you're having trouble, try giving

careful thought to the exact circumstances of your arrival. It's also possible that the portal will be in a remote, or difficult to access location. Fortunately, where there's one portal, there's probably at least a few others that can be tracked down with enough time and effort.

- If you arrived via summoning:
  - Your summoner (or another suitably powerful magician) may know a way to reverse the ritual and send you back home. Though, depending on the individual, you may have to rely on force or blackmail to get him to cooperate. Alternately, you can pretend to be so annoying and incompetent that he'll be begging to trade you in for a better model.
- If you died on Earth:
  - Being dead significantly reduces your odds of successfully returning to Earth as anything other than a corpse, but you can check with your god or goddess just in case.
- If you were reborn or reincarnated by a goddess:
  - Just ask her. Assuming she's the friendly sort, and there's no heavenly restrictions preventing her from doing so, she'll probably be willing to lend you a hand. But, you'd better hope that she doesn't accidentally drop you somewhere else by mistake.
- If you were reborn or reincarnated by a god:
  - Don't get your hopes up. He's almost certainly either too incompetent to pull it off correctly, or too determined to see you suffer to ever consider helping. In the case of the latter, you could try sucking up to him with your deeds and prayers, but even that might only be enough to avoid having your equipment blow up in your face.
- If you're trapped in a true video game world:
  - Try taking off your VR equipment, or just flail around until you smash the PC or game console entirely. If the shock doesn't kill you outright, or turn you into a drooling vegetable, you're free.
- If you're in a dark fantasy world:
  - It never hurts to try any of the above options, but potential escape routes in dark fantasy really only exist to give you a small measure of hope before crushing it in the cold, heartless grip of agony and despair. And if you actually do manage to escape, don't be surprised if something follows you home…

- If you're really desperate:
  ○ When you're within hearing distance of the demon lord's minions, drop a few hints that you miss your world. When word gets back to him, he may offer you a free trip home just to get you out of his hair (or tentacles). Do note that there's at least a 50 percent chance that he's lying and the entire thing is a death trap, so prepare accordingly.
  ○ While not recommended, you could always try getting run over by a carriage, or whatever the local equivalent of a truck is, in hopes that you'll get reincarnated back on Earth. But, you're far more likely to end up in another fantasy world (the fantasyverse is designed in layers, like an onion), or just plain dead.

Cutting and Running

Returning to Earth is best done either immediately after arrival, or after completing your main quest. If you absolutely have to leave in the middle, try to time it so as not to leave either your party members, or the world as a whole, in especially dire straits. Wait until a time that's safe and convenient, then let your allies know what you're doing and why. Offer to help if there's any last favors they need before you go. If you don't, you're risking a massive karmic reprisal during your return trip.

At the same time, you want to be very careful to ensure that the enemy does not learn of your plans. While the dark emperor or demon lord might be glad enough to see you leave that he won't stand in your way, he may also decide that just conquering one world isn't nearly enough and follow you home. (In that case, we highly recommend *So You've Been Drafted to Fight Invaders, Possibly from Space*). Alternately, he might rush to destroy your escape routes to ensure that you have no way out. Either way, it's best to keep things quiet.

If you're able to consistently travel back and forth via portal, instead of simply leaving for good, you may want to take advantage of that fact to rest and resupply between adventures, or train in safety before a major battle. You can even bring back some presents from Earth for your party members and other allies. Studies have shown that chocolate, instant ramen, and Japanese manga (especially of the "naughtier" variety) are especially popular among natives of the fantasyverse. Though, no matter how careful you are, you will have to deal with the occasional

enemy (or clumsy ally) following you home and causing all sorts of trouble (dangerous or wacky). So, if the back-and-forth life doesn't appeal to
you, it's probably best to destroy, or at least seal off the portal to prevent
any future cross-world contamination.

Finally, keep in mind that, outside of the rare reliable portal, returning to Earth is often a one-way trip that marks the official end of your
fantasy world adventures. There probably won't be an opportunity for
regrets or second chances, so only leave if you're really, really sure.

The Best Souvenirs

Whether you're returning to Earth as a triumphant hero or a snivel-
ing coward, you may be tempted to try and bring something along with

**Having access to a reliable portal opens up all sorts of intriguing possibili-
ties. Just make sure nothing follows you home.**

you as a souvenir of your time in the fantasyverse. Sure there are the memories, the courage, the confidence, and all that other touchy-feely mental crap, but it's always nice to have something a bit more physical. While what makes for the "best" souvenirs is really a matter of personal preference, here are some of the most popular choices.

- A Ring or Pendant
  - Regardless of the type or design, this piece of jewelry is meant to serve as a memento of a friend or lover you left behind in the other world. While they generally serve no practical purpose on their own, items of this type may act as a beacon, allowing you or one of your younger relatives to be summoned back to the fantasyverse in the future. Alternately, if you brought an item of this type back from a dark fantasy world, you can give it to your worst enemy and hope the summons catches him instead.
- Your Favorite Weapon
  - Chances are the legendary sword of the gods would be put to

Sure, you may have doomed the world by taking off with the one weapon capable of killing the demon lord, but it really ties the room together.

much better use in the hands of a future hero, but it would also look really cool sitting on your mantle.

- Magic Artifacts
  - Although there's no guarantee that they'll work back on Earth, items that allow for magical storage, teleportation, the ability to understand any language, or even open a portal back to the world they're from can be extremely useful in your daily life.
- Solid Gold
  - Most fantasy worlds have yet to advance to the era of paper money, relying on gold, silver, and jewels for normal everyday transactions. And, while 15 gold coins might only be enough to buy you a crappy accessory in the fantasyverse, back on Earth you could use it to pay your rent for a year, buy the complete set of So You've guides, or hire a really good therapist (and, considering some of the fantasy worlds out there, you may need one).
- A Magical Pet
  - If you don't trust your party members to take care of your magical floating cat thingy, you can always bring it home with you, where it's guaranteed to be just as cute, fun, and/or annoying as it was back in the fantasyverse. Just be careful not to let too many other people see it, or you may find yourself being pursued by an army of dissection-happy scientists.
- Your Girlfriend or Boyfriend
  - After all the work you put in to building up your relationship, it would be a shame to let it end just because you have to return to Earth. Keep in mind that it's likely a one-way trip, and that your significant other will face a very steep learning curve adjusting to modern day life on Earth. But, it's nothing that can't be solved by the power of love and a copy of *So You've Been Pulled to Earth from a World of Monsters and Magic*.
- A Baby
  - If you're female, and you've progressed far enough along in one or more of your romantic relationships, you may find that your lover left you a final gift to remember him by. Children born and raised under these circumstances may manifest magical powers and abilities as they grow. Or, they might just end up with bright green hair. They're also highly likely to be summoned back to the fantasyverse at some point during their

teenage years to meet (and/or avenge) their father. You may
or may not be able to go along for the ride, so make sure your
little hero is properly trained and informed in preparation for
that day.

○ On the other hand, if you're male and your lover stayed behind
when you returned to Earth, it's quite possible that you're
the one who left her a special souvenir. So, don't be surprised
when, years later, a mysterious child appears, calls you daddy,
and begs you to come home. In fact, if you lack easy access to a
portal, leaving a pregnant wife or girlfriend behind is the most
reliable (though not exactly laudable) way to secure yourself an
eventual return ticket to the fantasyverse.

≋ 19 ≋

It's Never Over ...
Unless It Is

Assuming that you decided, or were forced, to go back to Earth after the conclusion of your adventures, what comes next? Returning to normal life might seem impossible after everything you've seen and done. There will be some adjustments, and you might not ever return to your "pre-adventure" version of normal. But don't worry, plenty of former heroes have found themselves in the same situation and gone on to live successful and fulfilling lives, so there's no reason that you can't do the same.

Returning to Normal(?) Life

If you were able to return to Earth the moment you left, give or take, you can avoid all the complex social and legal issues that would otherwise crop up. You just need to focus on the mental side of things. First and foremost, you'll want to quickly try and remember exactly where you were and what you were doing before you left for the fantasyverse. It may (literally) seem like a lifetime ago, but if you can manage to avoid any major slipups here, there's a much lower chance of a trip to the mental institution later on. If your memories are fuzzy, go ahead and fake a mild illness. Ideally, you should seem sick enough that a bit of minor disorientation is acceptable, but not so sick that you have to see a doctor. You can probably use the illness card to give yourself a couple of days to rest and gather your thoughts, but you really need to resume your old life, including school or work, as soon as possible. That will not only help your brain make the mental switch back from hero to zero, but also keep others from getting suspicious. If your mental age no longer

While going from office worker to heroic knight is a pretty jarring transition, the reverse can be just as bad.

matches your physical one, you'll have to do your best to act the age you look to avoid arousing suspicion, or winding up in juvenile detention for trying to order an ale in a 15-year-old's body. Of course, you don't have to remain a boring student or dreary office drone forever, but try and make sure any major skill increases and lifestyle changes (physical or mental) are done on a believably gradual timeline. Just because you're now strong enough to bench press a minivan or call lightning from the sky doesn't mean you should. You certainly don't want to have to deal with worried friends and relatives, interventions, or suspicious government agents pestering you for an explanation. The only exception to this rule is if the entire purpose of your fantasy world journey was to give you the necessary skills and/or character development to deal with a sudden crisis. In those cases, survival and success trumps caution.

If you've been gone from Earth for a long time, things start to get much more complicated. When you've been missing for days or weeks, you might be able to manage with a really good excuse and a lot of apologies. But as that time span stretches into months or years, it becomes increasingly difficult to come up with a viable cover story. Expect lots of interviews with not only family and friends, but police and psychiatrists as well. Creating an elaborate yet robust explanation for your unexplained absence is a bit beyond the scope of this guide. You could always say that you returned after five years as a master archer because you were stuck on a deserted island with nothing better to do, but that's likely a bit too cliché to be believable. If you need assistance, we recommend *So You've Found Yourself in Desperate Need of an Elaborate Cover Story*. Unfortunately, that's only the beginning. You're bound to find yourself impossibly far behind on your school and/or work (assuming you still have a job). Even worse, if you were gone for too long, you might find that you've been declared legally dead. In which case, convincing everyone (especially the government) that you're actually alive will be a long, complex, and emotionally draining process.

Eventually though, things will calm down, and that's when you can start reaping the benefits of your adventure in the fantasyverse. Gradually sell off the gold or other valuable items you brought back with you. Use your enhanced physical abilities to become a sports superstar. Put your cooking skills to use as a top chef. Get ahead in all parts of life with careful use of magic. Or, if you crave excitement, put your skills to use as a mercenary, superhero, or vampire hunter. You could even write a book about your adventures, or join the staff at So You've Guides to help with the next edition of this one. The possibilities are endless! While you should still do your best to keep your connection to the fantasyverse a secret (you never know who or what may be lurking nearby), there are enough other, more ordinary explanations for your sudden mastery of the broadsword that it's not very hard to keep the truth under wraps. So have fun and enjoy your new and improved normal.

How to Not Sound Crazy

If keeping such a big secret sounds like too much trouble, you could always take a page from a certain famous billionaire and loudly declare "I am a fantasy world hero!" If you're lucky, your bold proclamation will result in fame, fortune, and an endless stream of book and movie deals. However, unless you brought some sort of definitive proof back with you, it's much more likely that you find yourself in a padded cell being fitted for a new jacket. Feel free to take the risk if you want but, for most returned heroes, the first rule of visiting the fantasyverse is don't talk about the fantasyverse. As common as it is to end up in a fantasy world these days, most people will still assume you're crazy if you start telling them about your adventures. You also want to avoid obsessing over everyday objects like plumbing, refrigerators, and smartphones no matter how much you missed them while you were gone.

For those returning from video game worlds, keep in mind that Earth lacks status screens, and that most people don't go around talking about how they need to earn 255 more EXP to go up another LVL and

Unless you want to be labeled as crazy or, even worse, an MMO junkie, try not to talk about stats and leveling in public.

cap their INT in order to gain a bonus skill point to boost their CRIT rate. If the average person hears that, they'll either think you're crazy, a nerd, or both. You won't be able to enter everyone's houses and take the healing potions they have lying around in their showers either. Remember, Earth doesn't have any NPCs ... or does it?

Needless to say, Earth features considerably less monsters than the average fantasy world, so don't walk around everywhere with a giant sword or any other obvious weapons. Armor, while less likely to get you arrested, is similarly a no-go. You also don't need to run for cover every time a large shadow passes overhead. It's probably just a bird, a plane, or maybe even Superman. Either way, it's certainly not a blood-thirsty chaos dragon ... probably. (So You've Guides cannot be held liable if you are maimed, eaten, or otherwise killed by a chaos dragon due to following this advice.) If you are legitimately threatened, it's best to use violence only as a last resort and even then, hold back as much as possible. Don't go cutting down someone's overly aggressive pet dog, or frying a pickpocket with your biggest fireball. You won't get any EXP, and you may very well find yourself in considerable legal trouble.

Prepping the Next Generation

Keep in mind that any younger family members you may have, especially children, nieces, nephews, and grandchildren are considerably more likely to be sent to the fantasyverse than the average person. This is especially true if they show a special interest in your adventures and/or souvenirs. As a veteran adventurer, it's only right that you help prepare them for their own journeys. Whether or not to actually tell them that fantasy worlds are real is best left to your own discretion, as some people simply refuse to believe until they see it with their own eyes. But, even if you have to frame your tales as fiction, all that information is bound to help them hit the ground running once they arrive. You should also make sure that your younger relatives have the basic physical and mental skills needed to succeed in another world. But don't stop there. Be a friend, play some video games, beat on each other with wooden swords. Even helping them create survival packs can make for a wonderful bonding experience.

Throughout all of this, try to make sure that you don't go too far. While it doesn't hurt if your young protégé ends up a bit overprepared, you don't want to become a full-on mentor. As previously discussed, the mentor role drastically increases your chances of death should you ever return to the fantasyverse. You're far better off being that cool, but slightly odd relative who likes to tell crazy stories.

Most importantly of all, remember that this book, and *So You've* guides in general, make the perfect gifts for birthdays, bar mitzvahs, Christmas, Chanukah, Festivus, Decemberween, Life Day, and any other special occasion. They even come in a convenient box set (*So You've Decided to Purchase Every Single So You've Guide*) in case

Nothing says "I love you" like giving your friends and family the complete set of So You've Guides.

you want to make certain that your future hero is truly prepared for anything.

One Last Round

Just because your adventure is over doesn't mean that there won't be another one down the road. Once you've been to the fantasyverse, even if you failed your quest, there's always a chance that you'll be called back. Perhaps a new evil has risen (they tend to do that), and the goddess in charge decided that she'd rather deal with a hero she already knows. Maybe the friends or lover you left behind have been desperately searching for a way to bring you back. Or, there's always the chance that your rival or arch enemy will summon you as part of a complicated revenge scheme.

Return trips are by no means guaranteed and they don't come immediately. You can normally expect a gap of anywhere from one year to several decades between adventures. Unfortunately, that's a very wide range, so there's really no choice but to live normally until the time comes. Make sure to keep your survival pack stocked and on hand and, of course, don't neglect your training. While there have been heroes who returned to the fantasyverse as overweight, out of shape slobs and still managed to work things out, it's far better to save yourself the embarrassment and painful emergency exercise regime and just stay fit at all times. Buff up those abs, don't forget leg day, and keep your fighting skill intact. It might not be easy to find people to practice your sword skills on, but there are communities for just about everything on the internet these days, so there's bound to be at least one for people who enjoy getting hit with a mace. It's a good idea to practice your magic as well. Whether or not the spells themselves work on Earth, you can at least review the words, forms, and the like. Even if you're never able to return to the fantasyverse, there's really no disadvantages to being physically fit and capable of impaling a burglar with a spear from the other side of the room, so all that training is a win-win either way.

Finally, if you want to increase your chances of returning to the fantasyverse, there are steps you can take.

- Leave a Child Behind
  - As covered in Chapter 18. However, if you've already returned to Earth, it's a bit too late to do anything about that.

- Research
  - ○ Conduct complex scientific and/or magical research into how to travel between worlds. This tends to be expensive, and flies at odds with not sounding crazy, but it often bears fruit eventually.
- Pray
  - ○ If you were originally summoned or reincarnated by a goddess, your heartfelt pleas (or constant nagging) may convince her to send you back.
- Find a Portal
  - ○ If you originally traveled via portal, closely monitor said portal for any signs of its reopening. If the portal has been destroyed or otherwise rendered inaccessible, search for others (see Chapter 1), there's usually at least a couple more out there somewhere.
- Have an Existential Crisis
  - ○ If your adventure was all about teaching you to grow and improve as a person, dial back a bit on the new and improved you. With a bit of luck, you may convince the fates that you need another round for the lesson to stick.
- Try Reverse Psychology
  - ○ Loudly and repeatedly declare how glad you are to be home, and how you never want to go on another adventure for as long as you live. This is especially likely to work if you returned from a comic fantasy world, as they love to milk your misery for laughs.
- Die
  - ○ As previously stated, So You've Guides *DOES NOT* recommend intentionally trying to invoke death as a means of traveling between worlds. Seriously, don't do it! The success rate is too inconsistent and, if anything, suicide or even intentional endangerment is likely to reduce your chances of making the cut. Besides, we don't want to have to deal with all legal fallout if there's a sudden spike of people being hit by trucks. (We already had way too much of that after the release of *So You've Been Trapped in a Dreamworld*.) Just keep the possibility of a trip to the fantasyverse in mind as a nice potential bonus after death, rather than something to aim for.

Finally, remember that even if you never return, you can be sure that your time in the fantasyverse will always remain a treasured memory, providing love, laughs, inspiration, and bragging rights. Congratulations, and enjoy the rest of your life!

Additional Research Material

While we at So You've Guides have worked hard to ensure that this book includes all the information needed for you to prepare for your stay in the fantasyverse, it never hurts to increase your general knowledge and genre-savviness. The best way to do so is to review the accounts of successful heroes who once found themselves whisked away to far off worlds. There are a surprising number of such records available, and they continue to grow. To aid in your research, the following list contains some of our most highly recommended chronicles of men and women who have been transported to, reborn in, or reincarnated into various fantasy worlds, along with a brief summary and some key lessons to be learned.

Alice in Wonderland/Alice's Adventures in Wonderland

As Told by: Lewis Carroll
Available as: EVERYTHING
World Type: Non-Standard Weird World
Summary: Alice follows a white rabbit into a bizarre world of endless tea parties, smoking caterpillars, killer playing cards, and math. Lots of drugs were probably involved.
Key Lessons:
- If something says "drink me," don't.
- Tea parties suck.
- Avoid murderous queens.
- Don't steal tarts.

Ascendance of a Bookworm

As Told by: Miya Kazuki
Available as: Novels, Anime, Manga
World Type: Standard Fantasy World
Summary: After getting crushed to death under a pile of books, Motosu is

reborn as a young girl in a medieval fantasy world where she makes it her life's goal to create more books (and hopefully some stronger shelves).

Key Lessons:
- Having an alternate victory condition.
- Remember to exercise.
- Try, try, again.
- Monetizing your knowledge.

Cautious Hero: The Hero Is Overpowered but Overly Cautious

As Told by: Light Tuchihi
Available as: Novels, Anime
World Type: Dark Fantasy World with Video Game Elements
Summary: A goddess who belongs in a comic fantasy world recruits a very powerful hero to save a doomed planet. He proceeds to drive her crazy by turning "be prepared" up to 11(thousand).
Key Lessons:
- Be careful.
- Be cautious.
- Be overly cautious.

The Chronicles of Narnia

As Told by: C.S. Lewis
Available as: Novels, Movies
World Type: Standard Fantasy World
Summary: Snotty British kids visit a world of talking animals where they learn important life lessons and thinly disguised Christian values over a series of heartwarming adventures.
Key Lessons:
- Portals are annoying.
- Don't take candy from strangers.
- Turkish delight isn't as good as it sounds.
- Christmas is awesome.
- Always trust lions.

A Connecticut Yankee in King Arthur's Court

As Told by: Mark Twain
Available as: Novel
World Type: Standard Fantasy World Set in the Past
Summary: A 19th-century engineer ends up in ancient Camelot, displaces Merlin, and starts the industrial revolution a bit too early before it all blows up in his face.

Key Lessons:
- The power of SCIENCE!
- Know your history and mythology.
- Pace yourself.
- Don't doubt magic.

Digimon Adventure/Digimon: Digital Monsters

As Told by: Reiko Yoshida
Available as: Anime, Manga, Video Games
World Type: Video Game-Style World
Summary: Seven children are whisked away to the digital world, and embark on an epic monster training adventure that's not at all the same as a certain other popular monster training franchise. Really.
Key Lessons:
- How to train your monster.
- Evolutions are awesome.
- Angels are overpowered.
- Digimon are the champions!

Do You Love Your Mom and Her Two-Hit Multi-Target Attacks?

As Told by: Dachima Inaka
Available as: Novels, Anime, Manga
World Type: True Video Game World
Summary: A high schooler is given the chance to beta test a brand new super realistic MMO. The only catch, his mom gets to come along and she's way more powerful than he is.
Key Lessons:
- Good moms are awesome.
- Evil moms are scary.
- Family relationships are complicated.
- Too many puns!

The Eminence in Shadow

As Told by: Daisuke Aizawa
Available as: Novels
World Type: Standard Fantasy World Leaning Dark
Summary: Upon being reborn in another world, Cid sets out to realize his lifelong dream of being the shadowy mastermind of a secret organization. He recruits some followers, makes up a ridiculous story about an evil cult, and sets out to have fun fighting against imaginary enemies. Turns out, it's all real and he's the only one who doesn't know.

Key Lessons:
- Trucks are magic?
- Having a secret identity.
- Life in the shadows.
- Being the mastermind.
- Extreme obliviousness.

Fushigi Yugi: The Mysterious Play

As Told by: Yuu Watase
Available as: Anime, Manga
World Type: Standard Fantasy World
Summary: High schooler Miaka enters a magical book and joins seven hot guys on a journey to summon a god who will grant her wishes. This makes her best friend extremely jealous.
Key Lessons:
- Everyone loves a summoned heroine.
- Best friends suck.
- The power of LOVE!
- Food is distracting.

Gate

As Told by: Takumi Yanai
Available as: Novels, Anime, Manga
World Type: Standard Fantasy World
Summary: After a large portal opens in Tokyo, a fantasy world army invades Japan and loses badly. Japan invades back. Meanwhile, ace soldier Yoji Itami gets all the girls.
Key Lessons:
- Japan rules.
- Guns > Swords
- Politics are a pain.
- Bring a tank.

How a Realist Hero Rebuilt the Kingdom

As Told by: Dojyomaru
Available as: Novels, Anime, Manga
World Type: Standard Fantasy World
Summary: Kazuya is summoned to fight the demon lord, but ends up being appointed king instead due to his incredible ability to do three times as much paperwork as a normal person.
Key Lessons:
- Don't skip civics class.
- Diplomacy over violence.

- Building a royal harem.
- It's good to be the king.

Inuyasha

As Told by: Rumiko Takahashi
Available as: Anime, Manga
World Type: Standard Fantasy World Set in the Past
Summary: Kagome travels to the past and fights demons alongside an infuriating dog boy who you know she'll fall in love with eventually.
Key Lessons:
- The past is magic!
- Being the supporting character.
- Ninja are awesome.
- Monks are perverted.
- Dog boys are hot.

Jumanji: Welcome to the Jungle

As Told by: Chris McKenna
Available as: Movie
World Type: True Video Game World
Summary: A group of high school students are pulled into a bad jungle adventure game and stuck in wildly mismatched avatars. Fortunately, extra lives are a thing.
Key Lessons:
- Avoid suspicious game consoles.
- Body swapping is fun ... if you get the right character.
- Hippos are hungry.
- Cake kills.

Konosuba: God's Blessing on This Wonderful World

As Told by: Natsume Akatsuki
Available as: Novels, Anime
World Type: Comic Fantasy World with Video Game Elements
Summary: After an embarrassing death, Kazuma is sent to a fantasy world where he proceeds to recruit the worst party ever.
Key Lessons:
- Goddesses make terrible boons.
- Choose your party wisely.
- The quest will find you.
- There's no such thing as a useless skill.
- Beware the giant toads.

Additional Research Material

Overlord

As Told by: Kugane Maruyama
Available as: Novels, Anime, Manga
World Type: Standard Fantasy World Turning Dark
Summary: A VR MMO player gets sent to a fantasy world as his skeletal avatar, along with his giant tomb and army of servants. He then goes on to conquer the world via a mixture of sheer power, good timing, and assorted misunderstandings.
Key Lessons:
- Choose your avatar carefully.
- Being the villain (sort of).
- Undead are useful.
- Faking it.

Parallel Paradise

As Told by: Lynn Okamoto
Available as: Manga
World Type: Disguised Dark Fantasy World
Summary: Youta falls out a window and awakens as the only man in paradise full of attractive young women, which is totally not a disguised hellscape run by murderous cults, psychopathic stalkers, and depraved dark gods … probably. Not safe for work, school, or anywhere that anyone else could possibly see you reading it.
Key Lessons:
- Fantasy world romance is easy.
- Things are never what they appear.
- If it seems too good to be true…

Reborn as a Vending Machine, Now I Wander the Dungeon

As Told by: Hirukuma
Available as: Novels
World Type: Standard Fantasy World with Video Game Elements
Summary: A man with a strange hobby gets reborn as a vending machine in a monster-filled dungeon. He soon teams up with a cute girl to squash monsters and sell soda.
Key Lessons:
- Don't die in a weird way.
- Being an inanimate object.
- It's always a cute girl.
- Use your abilities creatively.
- Everyone loves Japanese vending machines.

Re: Zero—Starting Life in Another World

As Told by: Tappei Nagatsuki
Available as: Novels, Anime, Manga
World Type: Dark Fantasy World
Summary: Subaru arrives in a fantasy world, meets cute girls, then dies repeatedly.
Key Lessons:
- The *Groundhog Day* effect.
- Witches suck.
- The importance of mental fortitude.
- Know your enemy.
- Cute maids are awesome (and deadly).

Reincarnated as a Sword

As Told by: Yuu Tanaka
Available as: Novels
World Type: Standard Fantasy World with Video Game Elements
Summary: Some random guy gets reborn as a magic sword, and teams up with a cute cat girl to slay monsters and cook curry.
Key Lessons:
- Being an inanimate object.
- The adventurer life.
- Cat girls are cute.
- Cooking saves the day.

Rising of the Shield Hero

As Told by: Aneko Yusagi
Available as: Novels, Anime, Manga
World Type: Standard Fantasy World with Video Game Elements
Summary: Four young men are summoned to a fantasy world and given legendary weapons. Naofumi gets stuck with the shield. His luck only gets worse from there.
Key Lessons:
- Shields are surprisingly awesome.
- Never trust the second-in-command.
- Don't be a jerk.
- Control your inner darkness.
- Everyone loves raccoon girls.

The Saga of Tanya the Evil

As Told by: Carlo Zen
Available as: Novels, Anime, Manga
World Type: Dark Fantasy World

Summary: A ruthless office worker denies the god of reincarnation to his face, and soon realizes that was a very bad idea.
Key Lessons:
- Don't diss gods.
- Magic war is hell.
- Little girls are scary.
- It can always get worse.

So I'm a Spider, So What?

As Told by: Okina Baba
Available as: Novels, Anime, Manga
World Type: Dark Fantasy World with Video Game Elements
Summary: After her classroom is destroyed in a mysterious incident, one girl is reborn as a spider monster in the midst of a deadly labyrinth. Her classmate is reborn as a handsome prince. Turns out, she got the better end of the deal.
Key Lessons:
- Spiders are cool.
- Creativity and planning for the win.
- Not all skills are good.
- Trust no one.

Spirited Away

As Told by: Hayao Miyazaki
Available as: Movie
World Type: Standard Fantasy World
Summary: Chihiro's parents literally pig out at a mysterious carnival, forcing their young daughter to work at a magic bathhouse to earn their freedom.
Key Lessons:
- Having an alternate victory condition.
- Mysterious food is dangerous.
- Remember your name.
- Don't judge a giant blob monster by appearances.

Sword Art Online

As Told by: Reki Kawahara
Available as: Novels, Anime, Manga
World Type: True Video Game World
Summary: 10,000 players are trapped in a deadly VR MMO. Beta-tester Kirito ends up saving the day with his swords and fangirls.
Key Lessons:
- Beta test everything.
- Take care of your real body.
- Dual wielding for the win.

- Don't underestimate your love interest.
- It's never over.

That Time I Got Reincarnated as a Slime

As Told by: Fuse
Available as: Novels, Anime, Manga
World Type: Standard Fantasy World
Summary: A hapless office worker gets reborn as an insanely overpowered blue blob and decides to build his own kingdom.
Key Lessons:
- Being a monster.
- Power + Diplomacy = Victory
- Appointing the right people.
- Don't underestimate slimes.

The Vision of Escaflowne

As Told by: Hajime Yatate, Shoji Kawamori
Available as: Anime, Manga
World Type: Standard Fantasy World
Summary: Hitomi is whisked away to the world of Gaea, where she uses her fortune telling abilities and short skirt to charm hot guys piloting magic robots.
Key Lessons:
- Always carry a magic pendant.
- Being the supporting character.
- Mechs are magical.
- Be careful what you wish for.

The Wizard of Oz/The Wonderful Wizard of Oz

As Told by: L. Frank Baum
Available as: EVERYTHING
World Type: Non-Standard Weird World
Summary: Dorothy and friends sing and dance their way through the magical land of Oz, while simultaneously wiping out a full 50 percent of its witch population.
Key Lessons:
- Singing makes everything better.
- Witches are water-soluble.
- Wizards are overrated.
- It was inside you all along.
- There's no place like home.

Index

Numbers in ***bold italics*** indicate pages with photos

adventure xi, 1–177
adventurer 26, 48–49, 52, 76, 79, 90, 92, 105, 107, 144, 148, 164, 175
armor 18–19, 38, 65–67, 93, 126, 133, 151, 164
asshole *see* jerk
avatar 6, 10, 12, 23, 29, 34, 38, 49, 80, 108, 173–174

baby 23, 38, 158
big bad whatever *see* villain
body 6–7, 9–11, 13, 17, 19, 22–24, 29, 38, 90, 106, 120, 148, 141, 144, 147, 161, 173, 176; *see also* gender swap
boon (as a gift from a diety) 16–21, 22, 38, 46, 48–49, 60, 66, 173
boyfriend *see* love interest

cat girl 1, 27, 46, 128, 175
cell phone 14–15, 53, ***63, 14***3, 163
chocolate *see* food
class (as a job) 10, 19, 38, 48–54, 56, 59–60, 66–67, 71, 76, 81, 105, 107
cliché i–177
clothes 12–14, 22, 39, 52, 62, 64, 90, 97–***98, 11***6; *see also* fanservice
comedy *see* comic fantasy world
comic fantasy world 27–28, 35, 44, 60, 62, 80, 91, 95–102, 125–126, 128–129, 167, 170, 173
cooking *see* food
crafting 57, 63, 66–***68, 15***0; *see also* equipment
curry *see* food
cute thing 37, 77, 80–81; *see also* useless
cute weapon girl 136–***137; see also* run away!

dark fantasy world 28, 30–33, 35, 38–39, 55, 67, 74, 79, 91, 112–121, 126, 128, 139, 150, 154, 157, 170, 174–176; *see also* death, madness
dark lord *see* villain
death 7–8, 12, 30, 32, 39–40, 41, 45–46, 52, 96, 101–103, 114, 117, 121, 126, 145, 152–153, 155, 165, 167, 169, 173
demon lord *see* villain

Earth (as a planet) 1–3, 6, 8, 11–13, 22, 26–29, 31, 33, 37–39, ***42, 44***, 46–47, 48, 58, 63, 69–70, 73–4, 85, 88, 90, 93–95, 99, 100, 104, 107–108, 114, 123–124, 130–131, 135–136, 142–143, 145–150, 153–154, 156, 158–159, 160, 162–164, 166
eldritch horrors 119, 136, 141, 150; *see also* madness; run away!
equipment *see* weapon, armor
evil 4–5, 11, 1824, 27, 45, 46–47, 48, 53–54, 71, 83, 85, 90–92, 96, ***109, 11***6, 118–119, 121–122, 127, 130, 138–142, 144, 145, 150, 152, 166, 171, 175; *see also* villain
evil emperor *see* villain
EXP (experience points) *see* video game fantasy world

fan disservice 28, 100
fanservice 12, 28, 77, 84, 97–98, 100, 125
fantasyverse i–177
food 14, 16, 22, 28, 36, 44, 48, 53–54, 56–57, 62, 66, 69, 90, 93–***94, 97***, 110, 130, 135–136, 143–145, 146, 153, 155, 162, 172, 175–176

game elements 29–30, 49, 67, 89, 104, 170, 173–174, 176

Index

gender swap 7, 10, 23
genre-savviness 11–12, 28, 55, 85, 86,
    91–92, 95–96, 109, 126, 144, 149, 169
giant robot *see* mech
girlfriend *see* love interest
god 7, 16, 21, 32, 34, 57, 53, 61, 72, 80,
    88–89, 108, 114, 119–120, 136, 154, 157,
    172–174, 176
goddess 16–18, 20–21, 23, 36, 38, 49, 55,
    67, 80, 88, 138, 145, 149, 154, 166–167,
    170, 173
gold 2, 10, 15, 37–38, 65, 75–76, 78–79,
    90, 122, 125, 150, 158, 162

harem 15, 80, 100, 123, 127–129,
    131, 142, 145, 148, 173; *see also* love
    interest
hero i-177
hottie *see* love interest

inanimate object 25, 42, 105, 114,
    174–175

jerk 2, 44, 46, 53, 81, 83, 95
joke *see* comic fantasy world

king 3, 16, 18, 88, 93, 120, 131–133, 142,
    169–170, 172–173
kingdom 11, 22, 27, 48, 88, 90, 92, 125,
    130–137, 138, 145, 172, 177

level (as a power level gained via EXP)
    see video game fantasy world
love interest 3, 16, 41, 43–45, 75–76, 78,
    101, 118, 120, 122–125, 126–127, 129,
    139n-140, 157–159, 166, 177; *see also*
    harem
lover *see* love interest

madness 117, 119
magic i-177
material *see* crafting
mayonnaise *see* food
mech (as a robot that really shouldn't
    be in a fantasy world) 71–72, 135,
    177
mentor 11, 36–37, 86, 151–152, 164–165;
    see also cute thing
monster 14, 18, 22, 24, 27, 30, 32, 37,
    39–40, 45–46, 48, 52–53, 55, 57, 63,
    65–70, 89–92, 105–106, 114, 117, 119,
    125, 127–128, 131, 133, 135–136, 138,
    143–144, 145, 151–152, 158, 164, 171,
    174–177

mother xii, 16–*17, 74,* 85, 171
mysterious relative 2, 165

naked 13, 19, 80, 97, 117, 146

OP (overpowered) 10, 34–36, 39, 102,
    131–132, 139, 170–171, 177

paladin *see* asshole
party (as a group of people) 1, 10, 14–15,
    35, 41, 45–46, 51–56, 60, 62, 66–67,
    69, 73–85, 91–93, 96–102, 106–107,
    118, 120, 122, 132–133, 138, 140–143,
    149, 152, 155, 158, 173
pervert 80, 84, 102, 124, 173; *see also* fan
    disservice; fanservice
pet 67, 69–70, 97, 100, 143, 158. 164
pizza *see* food
portal 3–6, 15, 22, 41, 89, 113–114, 138,
    145, 149, 153–156, 158–159, 167, 170,
    172

queen *see* king

reborn 2, 7, 12, 21, 24, 36, 38, 114,
    138, 154, 169–171, 174–177; *see also*
    reincarnated
reincarnated 1, 7–8, 12, 21, 22, 25, 39, 41,
    54–55, 65, 73, 77, 89, 103, 111, 114, 116,
    123, 130, 154–155, 167, 169, 175–177;
    see also reborn
run away! 4, 40, 51, 56, 82, 84, 91, 101–
    *102, 11*3–114, 136–*137*

science *see* SCIENCE!
SCIENCE! 5–6, 11, 14, 22, 28, 68, 72,
    135, 171
second-in-command *see* traitor
shameless self-promotion *see* So You've
    Guides
skill 6–7, 11, 17, 19–20, 23, 29, 34, 39, 43,
    45, 48–56, 58–60, 65, 68–69, 71, 80–
    82, 84, 86, 88, 90–91, 102, 105, 108, 111,
    123, 130–131, 134, 138–139, 143, 146,
    151, 161–162, 164, 166, 173, 176
So You've Guides (company and series of
    books) ix-xii, 3, 5, 6, 14, 26, 47, 57, 71,
    95, 103, 112n, 124, 155, 158, 162, 164–
    165, 167, 169
spell (as the magical variety) *see* magic
standard fantasy world 26–27, 31, 35,
    86–94, 169–177
summon (as a spell) xi, 1, 5–6, 9, 11–
    12, 14, 16–17, 22–23, 28, 30–31, 34,

Index

36, 38–39, 41, 46, 49, 52–54, 58, 65, 69, 71, 73, 77, 83, 88–89, 103, 107, 111, 114, 116, 119, 123, 130, 136, 138, 141, 146, 154, 157–158, 166–167, 172, 175–176
supporting character 26, 41–46, 56–57, 126, 173, 177

training 9–11, 19, 24, 37, 39, 48–50, 53–54, 57, 67–71, 89–91, 102, 105, 126, 133–134, 138–139, 141, 150–152, 155, 159, 166, 171
traitor 12, 84–85, 91–93, 127, 133, 144, 175
transported 6–7, 10, 30, 169
treasure 1, 65–66, 110, 125, 141, 149
truck 7, 148, 155, 167, 172; see also death
true power 12, 139–141

useless see cute thing

vending machine 8, 148, 174
video game 6, 12, 15, 28, 36, 59, 104, 164
video game fantasy world 6, 10, 12, 23, 26, 28–30, 34, 38, 49, 55, 59–60, 67, 89–90, 95, 103–111, 126, 139, 143, 151, 154 163–164, 171 173, 176; see also game elements
villain 2, 18, 20, 24, 27–28, 32, 37, 43–44, 46–47, 59, 62, 67, 71, 76, 87–88, 90, 92, 96, 101, 110, 116–119, 120–122, 125–127, 128, 133, 138, 142, 144, 150, 174

war 130, 134, 136–137, 176
weapon 10, 14, 18–20, 32, 38–39, 46, 49–50, 54, 65–67, 89, 101, 104, 116, 118–119, 133–134, 136, 149, 151–152, 155, *157, 164*, 172, 175

zombie 6, 118, 148